Diane & Peter Swan, 2012
Published by Meserani Publishing
www.meseraniproject.co.uk

A CIP catalogue record for this book is available from the British Library.

ISBN 978-0-9575134-0-2

Cover design by Clare Brayshaw

*For those who are touched by
the beauty and magic of Africa.*

Contents

Foreword

There is something about Africa. It has a magnetic allure to its exotic life and landscapes like nowhere else on Earth and for many of us this is epitomised by the notion of a *safari*. The word derives from Arabic and means "to travel overland on a hunting expedition" and up until recently it was perfectly applied, although thankfully now most of us are hunting with cameras and it is no longer a preserve of the privileged few. Thus if we are lucky we find ourselves holidaying in a foreign land in search of an unfamiliar fauna, and while there is no mistaking a giraffe or a zebra or a lion, there are many less known species to confound and confuse you, particularly the plethora of antelopes!

This guide provides the perfect introduction to the most frequently encountered creatures and supplements everything about their behaviour and ecologies that you have forgotten from your armchair TV safaris, with a useful overview of their biology. It's accessible, easy to use, concise and has plenty of little nuggets of interest and importance. For instance, how do you tell a male from a female giraffe? Well, it's down to their *ossicones*, or horns, the males being bald on account of them being worn down when fighting. Imagine how good you would feel beating the guide to that little gem when one of your party asks the question!

But there is one frequently overlooked paradox when it comes to going on a safari, and that is that you will see and enjoy far more than most Africans ever will. Only a tiny percentage of African children ever see lions or giraffes, and worse, many live in a poverty we cannot imagine. The proceeds from the sale of this book will help address this by supporting the Meserani Project based in the notorious Kibera slum outside Nairobi. The plan is to re-build a school and the work will be overseen by the staff, pupils, parents and friends of Acklam Grange School in Middlesbrough. I've been to Kibera myself, I've seen and smelled it, had a brief taste of utter desperation, and that's why I am so keen to support the project.

So take this book on safari, learn a lot about the exciting animals you find and be comforted by the fact that as well as taking great memories home from Africa you are putting a little back too, a little that will mean a lot to people with next to nothing.

Chris Packham
BBC Wildlife
Presenter

The Authors

As regular independent travellers to Kenya and Tanzania, Diane and Peter Swan have established many contacts in both countries. They are both experienced at bush camping in the wild, and have trekked in many remote areas, sometimes using donkeys to transport their camping equipment on the longer expeditions. Peter has independently led several large groups of students on three week expeditions in the areas covered by the book, and has received several regional and international awards for the work he has done in this respect. Diane has devoted her time to consolidating the authors' personal knowledge through thorough and critical research.

All pictures in the book have been taken by the authors and their friends – thus ensuring that they are authentic examples of what tourists on safari can expect to take.

Diane and Peter run a UK registered charity, The Meserani Project, which supports deprived schools and schoolchildren in Kenya and Tanzania. At the time of print the project has rebuilt three primary schools in Tanzania, sponsored many pupils from these schools to go through secondary education, provided food and resources to young people in the Kibera Slum, Nairobi, and is currently supporting a school in the Kibera Slum. All profits from the sale of their book will go directly to this project.

Introduction

As two independent travellers who have developed a passion for East Africa, we have derived great pleasure from sharing our experiences with a wide audience, whether it be friends and family, or groups of students that we have led on expeditions throughout Kenya and Tanzania. This book provides us with the opportunity to reach an even wider audience. Moreover, what we hope our book provides you with is something that we have found missing throughout all our visits to the game parks and reserves of Kenya and Tanzania, quite frustratingly so – and that is a guide that makes your animal sightings more meaningful and authentic, and makes your experiences more complete and wholesome rather than just a fleeting visual experience.

We would like to make it clear to you right at the outset that it is not a travel guide to East Africa—there are plenty of these in existence, many of them are excellent, and we would not wish to compete with them. Indeed, later on we will recommend to you those that we feel would be most worthy of your consideration. However, it would be remiss of us not to provide you with some 'insider tips' based on our own travelling experiences, and offering insights into opportunities available to travellers in Kenya and Tanzania that may not be covered in the traditional travel guides – see the *Insider Tips* section near the end of the book.

Some travellers to East Africa that we come across have the "tick the box" mentality, whereby the main aim is to take photographs of any animal they encounter, as quickly as possible, and then move on to the next one. Knowledge is irrelevant to them, it is the photograph that is the key – to impressing their families and friends back home. The moment that switched us from this mentality was the morning we turned off the engine of our 4x4 vehicle on the banks of the Tarangire River, and just sat for about 30 minutes sharing the lives of a small herd of elephants as they searched for water in the virtually dry river bed. It was an amazing experience just listening to nothing else but the sounds they were making, and feeling extremely privileged to be the only people in the world who were sharing their personal time with them. As we watched their behaviour, and shared some of their peace and tranquillity away from the convoys of four-wheel drive vehicles, we realised what we had been missing on all our previous mass-tourism safaris. The next thing that hit us was the realisation that we didn't actually understand much of their behaviour, and we felt that this experience we were sharing with them would have

been so much more meaningful if we had some background knowledge on their diet, habitat and communication. In the days that followed, and as we began to share more and more quality time with the wildlife of Kenya and Tanzania, the idea behind this book began to take shape.

We have included what we believe to be the thirty most popular animals to be found in Kenya and Tanzania, as well as eight interesting reptiles you are likely to encounter and four large birds. There is an entire chapter devoted to each, with an abundance of interesting and useful facts such as identification, behaviour, communication, predators and threats to survival. Physiology, habitat, location, diet and reproduction are also covered in a concise and easy-to-read style. Full colour photographs are included in every chapter to help you with identification, and we believe it is worth mentioning that these are 'real' photographs, in that they were taken by us or by friends while on safari in Kenya or Tanzania. As such they are typical of the kind of photograph that you yourself are capable of taking.

Further chapters cover national parks and game reserves, landscapes, climate and migration, and there are anecdotal notes within many chapters giving more information to further enhance your safari experience. Our invaluable *Insider Tips* deserve a whole chapter to themselves, and we hope very much that you will find something here that will provide as much pleasure and inner satisfaction as we ourselves have experienced throughout our travels.

Finally, and most importantly, we would like you to know that every single penny we make from the sale of this book will go towards the Meserani Project, a project set up by Acklam Grange School in Middlesbrough with the sole aim of changing the lives of young people in East Africa. The project has direct links with eight schools in Kenya and Tanzania, one of them inside Africa's largest slum at Kibera in Nairobi, and offers support and resources for these schools. Three primary schools have already been rebuilt and eighty-six pupils from primary schools in the Meserani region of Tanzania have been funded to attend secondary school. On behalf of all the young people who have benefited from the Meserani Project, we thank you for buying this book—your money has been well spent!

National Parks, National Game Reserves, Private Conservancies, Wildlife Sanctuaries in Kenya and Tanzania

National Parks

National parks are acknowledged as large areas of land of outstanding natural beauty, and usually contain a wide variety of wild animals and birds that are living in their natural habitat. Some are renowned specifically for their flora and geographical features, it is therefore worthwhile doing your home work beforehand if you think you are going on a safari to observe wildlife, otherwise you may be disappointed. National parks are protected by the government and the public are allowed to visit them for a fee, usually quoted and paid for in US dollars. Residents' park entry fees are usually at a lower rate and are paid in the local currency.

Human habitation is strictly forbidden in national parks. Boundaries of national parks are not normally fenced so the animals are free to come and go as they please. While in the park the animals are protected, but once they leave the park they are fair game for poachers or locals.

National Game Reserves

National game reserves are usually found in close proximity to national parks. The land may be used for other purposes such as human habitation and grazing of domestic livestock.

Private Conservancies

Private conservancies are privately owned and funded, and are able to invest and work intensively on wildlife conservation projects, which may involve local communities.

Wildlife Sanctuaries

Wildlife Sanctuaries are areas that have been set aside by the government or private bodies to protect wildlife. Hunting, shooting and fishing is forbidden.

Kenya

In Kenya the national parks are maintained and administered by a government body, the Kenya Wildlife Service (KWS)—www.kws.org. National game reserves are administered by local councils.

Tanzania

In Tanzania the national parks are maintained and administered by the Tanzanian National Park Authority (Tanapa)—www.tanzaniaparks.com. The National Wildlife Game Reserves are a wildlife division of the Ministry of National Resources and Tourism. Nearly 25% of land in Tanzania is protected by national parks, game/hunting reserves and controlled zones. Tanzania currently has 12 national parks, 13 game reserves, 38 game controlled areas, 120 National Cultural Heritage Sites and the world-famous Ngorongoro Conservation Area.

Tanzania: Ngorongoro Conservation Area

The Ngorongoro Conservation Area is administered by the Ngorongoro Conservation Area Authority—www.ngorongorocrater.org
♦The Ngorongoro Crater is:
♦The world's largest unbroken and un-flooded caldera.
♦A UNESCO World Heritage Site.

The crater was formed two to three million years ago when a volcano erupted and subsequently collapsed in on itself. It is 19km in diameter and has walls that are 600m high, which actively discourages animals from migrating. It is home to 25,000-30,000 animals.

The Maasai are allowed to graze their cattle within the crater, but must enter and leave each day.

General Information

The wildlife that you are going in search of while on safari are not restricted to the parks and reserves. The animals are free to move in and out of the parks and reserves as they please in search of food, water and a mate, so always be on the lookout for photographic opportunities—and be mindful of personal safety!

Parks and reserves have designated times when you are allowed to enter and leave. Visitors are allowed in after 6 a.m. but must leave before 7 p.m. (check at the main gate where you enter). Passes for the parks and reserves are valid for 24 hours, but be aware that some passes become invalid once you exit through one of the gates, which means that you can't return even if it is within your 24 hour period—you will have to pay for another pass, or pay a reduced fee to re-enter.

A map of the park/reserve is useful and adds to the enjoyment of the visit. Buy the map at your earliest opportunity, which may be the camp site shop, hotel/lodge shop or the main gate. Do not bank on buying a map at the main gate as they may have sold out, and the parks/reserves can be very difficult to navigate if you do not know where you are! It is so easy to get lost! The map outlines the main tracks to be used in the dry and wet season with supporting information/diagrams about the wild life and flora.

Check that you are able to buy a pass for the park/reserve from the main gate. In some areas, which may be some distance away, you have to buy a card from a bank and deposit money into an account. You then present the card at the main gate and enter your pin number to purchase a 24-hour pass. You do not physically hand any money over. Make sure you can remember the pin number. The pass will have the time and date printed on it.

Retain the pass, this is checked by rangers as you enter the park/reserve, possibly when you are in the park/reserve and as you exit.

Be mindful of the time on a 24-hour pass. If you leave the park after the designated 24 hours is up you may be charged again for another 24 hours!

Always listen to, and adhere to the advice of the guides and park/reserve rangers. If you are an independent traveller ask them where the animals have been sighted that day.

When entering a park/reserve there is no guarantee you will see the animals listed. Some of the travel brochures, supporting information and guide books can be very vague! You may be told you will see antelopes or plains game, small mammals, medium-sized mammals etc., but which ones?

You need to be patient, alert and vigilant at all times. You may have to wait a long time before you see anything. But when you do it is well worth the wait. Turn the vehicle's engine off and just enjoy the moment for as long as you want. Sheer bliss.

It is strictly forbidden to leave the main tracks and go across country while in a park/reserve. If you are caught doing so you may be asked to leave the park/reserve.

Do not speed while in the park/reserve—do not drive at more than 30-50km/h. This is to avoid upsetting/harassing/stressing or harming the animals. The terrain can be extremely treacherous. Treat it with respect. The roads are uneven and have numerous potholes, it is so easy to have an accident and upturn a vehicle. This is not an environment in which to have an accident or break down. You technically cannot get out of the vehicle while in a park/reserve, and if you do, you could be at high risk of been injured by the animals. Make sure that you have your car hire company's telephone details and your mobile phone with a fully charged up battery. It is worth keeping the car hire company's contact details on the memory just in case you lose the paper copy.

Be careful when driving through water, in muddy areas or across salt flats you may get stuck and need towing out. This may cost!

Your vehicle is like a hide. The animals are extremely tolerant, dismissive of vehicles and to all intent and purpose you feel as though they cannot see you. This gives a false sense of security. Remain in your vehicle at all times, unless advised otherwise. In some parks/reserves you are allowed out at toilet spots, picnic spots or viewing points. One such picnic spot worth mentioning is the Ngoitokitok Spring Picnic Site in the Ngorongoro Crater. You are allowed out of the vehicle to toilet, stretch your legs and eat lunch. But beware, if you eat outside the safety of your vehicle you may be relieved of your lunch (and your hands) by the birds of prey who regularly swoop down on unsuspecting tourists.

Do not hang out of the windows of the vehicle to get closer to the animals or to get a better view/photograph either. The animals can recognise the human form and may sprint into action with amazing speed.

Do not be tempted to approach river banks or lakesides on foot, to dip your feet in the shallow waters or go for a swim to cool down. This is the natural habitat for crocodiles and hippos. You may not see them but they most certainly will see you, even though they are submerged under water and they will not think twice about attacking you.

Firearms are strictly forbidden in park/reserves.

Respect the Environment

The main gate clearly displays the rules and regulations that you have to observe while in the park/reserve. They are also written on the back of the ticket as a reminder. Like the Country Code that operates in national parks in the UK you are asked to respect the environment by not smoking, leaving any litter, food, cigarette tab ends behind, not to light fires or remove any plant material, animals, soil or rocks.

Respect the Wildlife

The animals seen on safari are in their natural habitat—they are wild, highly dangerous and unpredictable. On sighting an animal, switch off the vehicle's engine so that you do not to disturb or influence their behaviour and keep your distance. A minimum of 20m and 5 vehicles is recommended so as not to cause the animals any distress. Be considerate of other visitors in the park when travelling round the park and when observing the animals at close quarters. They too have paid a considerable amount of money to go on safari to see the wildlife.

When in close proximity to the animals avoid sudden movements that may startle and alarm them. Do not make any noises or gesticulate to gain their attention. The majority of the animals have excellent hearing so keep noise to absolute minimum. Talk quietly among yourselves and in some instances use sign language as a form of communication. Turn off the radio, cassettes, MP3 players, mobile phones (this includes preset reminders and alarms) and any jingles that start up digital cameras/watches.

If the animals are moving about, they have the right of way so do not obstruct them: allow them freedom of passage. It is particularly important not to get between a mother and her offspring. Females are very protective towards their offspring and are generally more nervous, agitated and aggressive than normal.

It is amazing how close you can get to the animals either in the jeep or at picnic sites and it is very tempting to attempt to touch and stroke them, as they are cute, have lots of appeal and appear to be very peaceful, very much like a domestic pet. But this is very deceptive. Do not touch the animals as they will most likely strike back. Children should be kept in check and told not to shout, torment or tease the animals.

Feeding the animals is strictly forbidden because they begin to associate humans with food and can cause problems. Baboons in particular can become a problem. Similarly do not leave food or the remains of food around campsites, on verandas or window ledges as it encourages the animals to come into close contact with you.

In the vicinity of monkeys/baboons it is advisable to lock the doors of the vehicle (whether or not you are in it) as they are more than able to manipulate the door handle and get inside.

Walking Safaris

Walking safaris and trekking holidays are becoming increasing popular with tourists and can either be pre-booked or when you arrive at your destination. Whatever you choose to do make sure you have the correct clothing and equipment with you and that you are physically fit for such an undertaking. You are in a hard, hostile, inhospitable, unforgiving environment fraught with danger 24 hours a day!

You will be under the guidance and supervision of a guide. You must listen and adhere to the advice of the guide at all times. Any deviation can put yourself or others in danger. Africa has an amazing, vast array of dangerous animals.

Animals are hard to track and find, so be patient. Be patient with your guide. Walk quietly behind the guide through the bush and keep talking to an absolute minimum. Be observant and aware of your surroundings, use your senses—sight and hearing.

As soon as you are walking in the bush, look around you, especially where there is dense vegetation, which is a prime place for the animals to rest in the midday sun when it is hot.

Areas with restricted visibility should be avoided as should steep-sided valleys, gullies, river beds and deep, steep-sided dense reed beds where you can become trapped with no escape route.

Animals are only aggressive if threatened, startled or provoked. If you do come face to face with an animal or a snake in the bush do not move. This will take a lot of nerve, but animals and snakes do associate anything that moves as prey. Keep still until they have moved on. We can, without realising it, indirectly communicate with some animals via our facial expressions and they may respond accordingly. Smiling and showing teeth is a sign of aggression, direct eye contact is challenging, and sudden movement indicates attack. Animals are especially dangerous during the mating season, when they are physically mating or where young are present.

Be careful when observing predators stalking prey or when they are feeding. Do not approach wounded animals, if they are traumatised they will behave and respond accordingly.

Whatever safari you choose to go on it is one big adventure that not many people get to experience. Enjoy!

15

Big Five

The "big five" is a term originally used by big game hunters who considered the elephant, rhinoceros (black & white), leopard, lion and buffalo as the most difficult and dangerous of all Africa's animals to track and hunt. This meant that they were highly prized among dedicated trophy hunters, whereas in the present climate where wildlife is protected, the big five are now regarded by tourists as top of their "must-see" list purely for photographic purposes.

Big Nine

The "big nine" has evolved as a recognised extension of the "big five" and includes the hippopotamus, zebra, giraffe and cheetah.

Our "Big Eleven"

African/Cape Buffalo
(Syncerus caffer)
Swahili: *Nyati/Mbogo*

Identification

The cape buffalo is a large heavily built animal with a cow-like appearance, and is one of Africa's "big five".

The head is large, and it has a short, thick neck and broad chest. It has small eyes protected by the horns. The large, droopy, fringed ears are also underneath the horns. The muzzle is wide and hairless, with moist nostrils. A prehensile tongue and broad incisors enable it to feed on tall, coarse grasses.

The cape buffalo's hide is extremely thick and protects it from thorny bushes and the penetrating claws of predators. The short, coarse, sparse coat, is grey-black in colour; this thins with age along with the appearance of bald patches.

Its limbs are strong, powerful and muscular with black splayed hooves. The front hooves are bigger than the rear hooves.

Both sexes have two low, rigid horns that grow out of the sides of the head and curve upwards. The male's horns, which are larger and thicker than the females, are joined by a shield (boss) that covers the entire forehead. The boss protects the skull of the male from serious injury when engaged in fighting.

The tail is long and has a tuft of hair on the tip.

Cape buffaloes have poor eyesight and hearing, but have an excellent sense of smell.

Head & Body Length:	2-3.5m
Shoulder Height:	1.4-1.7m
Tail Length:	0.75-1m
Weight:	500-900kg
Horn Length:	1.25m

Life Span
Sixteen to eighteen years in the wild.

Habitat

Cape buffaloes need a large area to roam around in, and are usually found in savannahs, grasslands, forests and woodlands. They can live at sea level or at altitudes of up to 4,000m, and are always found near water.

Behaviour

Cape buffaloes are sociable, non-territorial animals that live in large, mixed, stable herds/obstinacies of up to 1,500 individuals. The majority of the herd is composed of females (cows) and their offspring, surrounding the main herd are sub herds of bachelor males, sub herds of dominant males (bulls) and sub herds of females. The older bulls are to be found on the periphery. The majority of cape buffalos are docile and placid if left alone; serious fights are rare. When resting, they may lie down on the ground with their backs touching each other.

When threatened by predators, cape buffaloes form a tightly knit group, with the calves protected in the centre. This makes it hard for a predator to select, identify and isolate a suitable victim. Their cumbersome appearance is deceiving — although they cannot accelerate quickly, once they have gained momentum they can run at speeds of 57km/h and can easily outrun a lion. A lion attacking a buffalo risks a mob attack with the chance of been gored or trampled to death.

Old bulls usually live on their own, away from the safety and security of the herd. If disturbed, they can become unpredictable and highly dangerous. Solitary bulls are easy prey for lions.

During the dry season, when grass and water is in short supply, the herd disbands, regrouping again in the wet season. Undisturbed, they will graze continuously, but in the vicinity of humans and predators they prefer to feed in the early morning and evening. Making quick work of the food available, they are constantly on the move, searching for fresh food and water. Without a regular, plentiful supply of food and water, the cape buffalo's physical condition rapidly deteriorates, more than any other animal on the African savannah.

Cape buffalo are diurnal and nocturnal.

Diet

The cape buffalo is a herbivore and grazes on tall, coarse grasses. They need to drink water daily. During the dry season when food is in short supply they will eat the leaves from trees, shrubs and bushes.

Communication

Cape buffaloes are quiet, communicating with each other during the mating season by grunting and bellowing, and gently mooing to each other while eating. A calf in danger will bellow for its mother. They also use sight, scent and bodily postures to communicate.

Reproduction

Cape buffaloes are polygamous and breed all year round. The peak season for giving birth is during the rainy seasons. The dominant males mate with, and are protective towards the females. During the mating season they will search for females in oestrus by smelling and tasting their urine.

The gestation period is between 330-346 days. The female gives birth to a single calf, which remains hidden in thick undergrowth until it is able to follow and keep up with the herd. The calf has a thick, dense coat of brown-black hair, and is weaned by the time it is 12 months old. The bond between the female and the calf is strong and remains until the arrival of the next offspring, at which time the calf is chased away. Females remain with the maternal herd.

Cape buffaloes are sexually mature between three to five years old

Predators/Threats

Healthy cape buffaloes do not have any natural predators, apart from lions. The young, old, injured and diseased are easy prey for crocodiles, hyenas, and leopards. They are hunted for their meat and for sport by the trophy hunters. They can come into conflict with humans if they break fences, raid crops and are suspected of carrying bovine diseases. Loss of habitat and competition for food from domestic livestock threaten the cape buffalo's survival.

Trivia

♦The nickname for an old cape buffalo is "dagga boy".

♦Cape buffaloes are extremely dangerous and capable of killing any animal or human that stands in their way. If injured they will circle back and lie in wait for the perpetrator then strike when least expected.

♦Cape buffaloes suffer from heat stress and must drink twice a day.

♦Cape buffaloes have a strong musky smell.

♦Flies can lay their eggs in the horns of the cape buffalo. When the larvae hatch, they bore holes into the horns, which can seriously weaken and fracture the structure.

♦The cape buffalo's head and neck is extremely large, and it can take between 30 to 60 minutes for a lion to successfully suffocate or strangulate it. This is a long, slow and painful death.

♦Cape buffaloes have a weak immune system and are susceptible to bovine tuberculosis and foot and mouth disease. Tuberculosis is highly contagious and can rapidly decimate a herd of buffalo and their predators.

♦It is not advisable to domesticate the buffalo as it is unpredictable and highly dangerous.

♦The buffalo is immune to bovine sleeping sickness, which is carried by the tsetse fly.

African Elephant
(Loxodonta africana)
Swahili: *Tembo/Ndovo*

Identification

The African elephant is the world's largest land animal.

The rough, grey, sensitive, wrinkly skin which is 2.5-cm thick is almost hairless. There is a sparse covering of hair around the mouth, along the trunk and on the tip of the tail.

The head is large with a short neck and is supported by strong neck muscles. The eyes are small in comparison to its size. The head of the male elephant is rounded whereas the female's head is square.

The long, flexible, prehensile trunk acts as an extra limb and serves many purposes. It is used to breathe, smell, communicate, gather food, dig for water, suck up water, mud and dust, as well as lifting and gripping objects. In fact an elephant cannot survive without its trunk.

Two nostrils run the length of the trunk.

The elephant uses its trunk to siphon up water, which it then pours into its mouth and drinks. Mud or dust are also sucked up in a similar manner and then showered over the body to cool it down.

Two dextrous finger-like projections present on the tip of the trunk allow the elephant to grip small objects.

Both male and female elephants have two tusks made from ivory that continue to grow throughout their lives. The tusks differ in shape, size and angle and are used to identify individuals. The tusks serve many purposes: foraging for food, digging up tree roots, searching for water, stripping bark from trees, pushing trees over and fighting. Elephants, have a preference for either the right or left tusk, consequently one tusk wears out first or is damaged more than the other.

The elephant's teeth have evolved over time to cope with their coarse diet. They have four molars that have large grinding surfaces made up of many adjoining ridges/sections called laminae. The molars start growing at the back of the mouth and gradually move forwards to replace the old teeth as they fall out. They are replaced six times during the elephant's life. The absence of teeth in later life results in the elephant suffering from the effects of malnutrition and eventually dying from starvation.

The large, fan shaped ears are covered by a network of fine blood vessels close to the surface of the skin which dissipate heat and help to keep the elephant cool. Flapping of the ears also cools the elephant down. The skin on the ears is thin and delicate and easily torn by sharp thorns when foraging for food in the bushes, or when engaged in combat. These tear marks are used to identify individuals. Male elephants have more tears on their ears than females.

Four short, stocky legs sit directly beneath the large barrel-shaped body. Sponge-like cushions on the pads of the feet act as shock absorbers and allow the elephant to move silently through the bush. Toenails are present on the toes.

The tail is short and has a tassel of black hair on the tip.

Elephants have poor eyesight, excellent hearing and a keen sense of smell.

The male elephant is larger than the female.

Head & Body Length:	5-7.5m
Shoulder Height:	3-4m
Trunk Length:	2m
Tail Length:	1-1.5m
Weight:	2,268–6,400kg
Weight of Tusks:	22-45kg

Life Span
Up to 70 years in the wild.

Habitat
Elephants are usually found in savannahs, grasslands, woodlands and forests, where there is a plentiful supply of food and water.

Behaviour
Elephants are intelligent, sociable animals that live together in a small family group called a herd. The herd, which has a complex, hierarchical social structure based on age, is made up of 10 to 20 closely related individuals and consists of the matriarch (leader), 3-4 adult females, their offspring, newborn calves and adolescent males and females. If the herd gets too large it will split into two, one group

will be led by the older matriarch and the other will be led by a sister or cousin. It is extremely rare to find a female elephant alone. Males tend to be solitary but may live together in an all-male group.

Herds will temporarily merge during the wet season when food and water is plentiful. The herds disband during the dry season when they need to concentrate their efforts on searching for the dwindling supply of food and water. Walking at 6km/h they can cover large distances in their search for food.

Elephants spend 16 hours a day feeding, drinking, socialising, dusting themselves with fine dry soil and wallowing in mud to cool down. A combination of dried-on mud and dry soil acts as a sunscreen to protect the elephant's delicate skin, as well as serving as an exfoliator for dislodging ticks, flies and other parasites.

Elephants are particularly affectionate towards each other, using their trunks to greet and touch each other, as well as reinforcing old relationships. They also tend to and look after the old, sick and injured members of the herd.

Although gentle and peaceful animals, elephants can be extremely dangerous if they are wounded, sick or injured, or are protecting their young. They are more than capable of seriously injuring or killing anything that gets in their way.

Elephants mourn their dead by remaining close to them for several

days, by covering them with dirt, twigs, branches and leaves, and sensitively touching whatever remains with the tips of their trunks.

Elephants are diurnal and nocturnal. They rest at midday and sleep between 4-5 hours per night.

Diet

Elephants are herbivores and have a preference for fresh grass, but during the dry season when food is in short supply, they have to seek out alternatives. They are fortunate in that their size, strength and the presence of their trunk allows them to access sources of food that are normally inaccessible to other animals. They will uproot trees and shrubs, strip bark from the tree trunk, tear branches and twigs away from the tree, and reach up for fruit and seed pods. Elephants are destructive, and when present in large numbers they can put some

plant species at risk of extinction. In order to manage this delicately balanced ecosystem elephants may be translocated or culled by humans. The majority of the vegetation that the elephant eats is of poor nutritional value and they need to eat 200-300kg of food per day in order to survive. They produce 36kg of dung and 2,000 litres of methane per day. Elephants usually drink water daily, but when in short supply they can drink every second or third day. Water aids digestion and cools them down. Elephants can drink up to 189 litres of water a day.

Communication
Elephants use a variety of vocalisations, visual signals, bodily postures and their trunk to communicate with each other and their offspring. They are able to communicate infrasonically over 9km at low frequencies not audible to the human ear. They usually use this form of communication early morning or in the evening when it is cool.

Reproduction
Elephants breed any time of year.

Male elephants (bulls) come into musth in their mid to late twenties and begin to mate with the females when they are over thirty. Musth is a state of heightened sexual excitement and occurs at regular intervals, usually lasting from one week up to three to four months, with a nine-

month rest break during which time the bull will live alone. Bulls in musth are domineering, aggressive and unpredictable, and should be avoided. Older dominant bulls are able to remain in musth for longer periods.

When the bull enters musth the temporal glands above and behind the eyes increase in size causing the cheeks to swell, and a sticky fluid to continuously flow down either side of the face. A constant, strong smelling flow of dribbling urine is also present. The bull sends out low frequency calls to attract the attention of females. Following any female that responds to his calls, he will use his trunk to test if she is in oestrus. The male and female will  then spend some time sniffing one another before proceeding to mate. The older, larger and stronger bulls are more likely to succeed in mating with the females. Females also have a preference for older bulls.

Females (cows) give birth to their first born between the ages of 10 and 20 years old, and thereafter every 4-6 years. When resources are scarce and unable to sustain a high elephant population, the females can either alter their reproductive status so that they reach sexual maturity when they are older, or give birth less frequently. This increases the survival rate for them and their offspring. During years of drought the mortality rate for the calves can be as high as 50%.

Females come into oestrus during and after the rainy season. They are in oestrus for between 4-6 days, during which time they secrete a sticky fluid from the temporal gland down either side of their face.

Ninety-nine per cent of females give birth surrounded and protected by other females during the night. The gestation period is 22 months, with the female giving birth to a single calf. At birth the male and female calves are the same size. The males grow more rapidly, especially during their teens, and this continues throughout their lives. Females grow slowly and their growth ceases by the time they are 25 years old.

The calves are able to walk within 2-3 hours of being born and will spend the first few weeks of their lives lying down, resting and sleeping. Within two weeks, the pinkness behind the ears will have disappeared. Relying solely on their mother's milk, they suckle with their mouths from the two breasts that are located between the two front legs, usually for the first four months of their lives. They then begin to supplement their diet with soft green succulent grasses, progressing to the coarser grasses after 12 months. The calves continue to drink their mother's milk until they are 4-6 years old or until the next offspring arrives. For a short period of time the calves eat their parents' dung to establish essential micro organisms in their gut that aid digestion. Their tusks appear externally when they are 30 months old. Weaning is completed by the time the calf is five years old.

The calf is unable to control the two finger-like projections on the end of its trunk, necessary for grasping and manipulating objects, until it is six months old.

Playful and full of mischief, the calf has to learn basic motor coordination, behavioural and life skills from its mother in order to survive.

Females are fiercely protective and band together to protect their own and other females' calves. Juvenile females between two and eleven years old are attracted to, and will tend and care for small calves. This is known as "allo mothering" and increases the calves' chances of survival. Orphaned calves are looked after by lactating females. When threatened, the adults form a protective circle around the youngsters.

The female's reproductive life ceases between the ages of 45-50 years old. She will then spend the remainder of her life tending and caring for the young.

As the males begin to mature they will start to spend time away from the natal herd and will make the final break when they have reached sexual maturity at around 14 years old. This prevents in-breeding. During their teens they need the leadership of a matriarch and may latch onto a herd of females, but in their twenties they seek out the companionship of either younger or older males. They may also live a solitary life in isolation as an independent bull.

Females remain with the natal herd.

Predators/Threats

Elephants are illegally hunted by poachers for their tusks, and this is the main threat to their survival. The calves are natural prey for lions, hyenas, African wild dogs and crocodiles. Loss of habitat is also a threat to their survival.

Trivia

♦African elephants are larger than Asian elephants.

♦African elephants' ears are three times larger than Asian elephants and are shaped like the map of Africa! The African elephant's ears can grow up to 1.8m. Asian elephants' ears are small and rounded.

♦Asian elephants only have one finger-like projection on the tip of their trunk, and can only scoop objects up.

♦It is difficult to sex elephants as the male testes are internal.

♦Elephants stand up all of their lives, if they were to lie down they would suffocate.

♦*Musth* is an Urdu word that means "intoxicated".

♦Elephants are excellent swimmers.

♦Unlike Asian elephants, African elephants are not easily domesticated.

♦Male African elephants continue to grow throughout their lives and can reach more than 7,000kg in weight.

♦Female elephants can run faster than males.

Ivory

Ivory comes from the tusks of elephants, hippopotamuses, killer whales, narwhales, sperm whales, walruses and warthogs. Tusks are essentially teeth and are formed from layers of dentine.

The majority of ivory comes from elephants, from India as well as Africa. Elephant's tusks are the equivalent of upper, human incisors and continue to grow throughout their life. Subject to wear and tear and damage from fights, elephants can often be identified by the condition of their tusks alone. Despite the 1989 worldwide ban on the trade in ivory, the black market is alive and thriving. Poachers are willing to risk all to satisfy their client's insatiable desire and greed for ivory. The only way poachers are able to retrieve ivory from an elephant is by killing them, usually with a bullet, but occasionally by poisoning. The head has to be cut open, as 25% of the tusk is usually deeply embedded inside it. Once the tusk is removed, what remains is left to the scavengers.

Ivory has multiple uses: jewellery, cutlery, piano keys, furniture inlays, handles, billiard balls, religious objects, daggers, decorative boxes and works of art.

Trivia

♦The ivory from the tusks of the hippopotamus is of a different texture to that of the elephant, being denser and harder. It is usually used to make buttons, but has also been used to make false teeth.

♦The recent surge in the demand for ivory has seen the tusks of the stuffed heads of elephants and hippopotamuses being removed, usually as they go to auction. What was initially worth tens of thousands of pounds is suddenly worthless.

Black Rhinoceros
(*Diceros bicornis*)
Swahili: *Faru/Kifaru*

Identification

The black rhino is an odd-toed ungulate and has the reputation of being unpredictable, bad-tempered and aggressive.

The black rhino's thick, smooth, hairless skin is grey, but can be varying shades of brown if it has been wallowing in mud. The thick skin protects it from the thorns on the trees and bushes that it feeds on. The skin harbours parasites such as ticks, flies and crabs. It has no sweat glands. Hair is present on the fringes of the ears, on the tip of the short tail and as eyelashes.

The black rhino has a large, rotund body with a broad chest. Its legs are short and stumpy. It has three toes on hooved feet, and its footprint resembles the ace of spades.

The head is large with a long neck and an elongated face. It has a broad snout, large nostrils and a triangular, pointed, upper lip. Incisors and canine teeth are absent and it is heavily dependent on its prehensile muscular lips to grasp the twigs and leaves on the trees and bushes upon which it feeds. Two horns made of keratin sit centrally behind the nose. The horns have no bony skeletal attachment but actually grow from the skin and continue to grow throughout life. The anterior horn is longer than the posterior horn. Occasionally a third horn is present.

The black rhino's keen senses of smell and hearing compensate for its poor eyesight. The eyes are very small and are placed on either side of the head. In order to look straight ahead the rhino has to turn its head sideways. The black rhino is short sighted and cannot detect an immobile object at 30m. It can detect a moving object at 30-50m. The large, prominent, funnel-shaped ears are mobile and move independently of each other.

Males are slightly larger and heavier than females.

Head & Body Length:	3-4m
Shoulder Height:	1.4-1.7m
Tail Length:	50-70cm
Weight:	800-1,350kg

| **Horn:** | Anterior | 50cm-1.3m |
| | Posterior | 0.02-55cm |

Combined Weight: 6kg

Life Span
Forty years in the wild.

Habitat
Black rhinos are found in wooded areas such as woodlands, forests, shrub land and tropical bushlands. They can also be found in savannahs, grasslands and deserts. They like to be near water holes and mud wallows.

Behaviour
The black rhino is not very territorial and may have home ranges that overlap. The perimeter is scent marked at regular intervals with urine and communal dung heaps or middens. Urine is sprayed backwards at great force in the direction of bushes and trees.

Black rhinos have a solitary existence except when mating and raising offspring. They display little or no aggression towards each other. Despite its cumbersome appearance the black rhino is surprisingly agile and can run at speeds of up to 50km/h.

The black rhino is more nocturnal than diurnal, browsing on food early morning and evening and during the night. During the day it likes to rest and wallow in mud, which serves to cool it down. Dried mud acts as a sun screen and exfoliator as well as helping to deter ticks, flies and other parasites.

Diet
The black rhino is a herbivore and a heavy browser, feeding on branches, twigs, leaves, fruit, buds of woody plants and bushes, as well as small seedlings and herbs. It is capable of uprooting small bushes and shrubs and digesting thorns.

The black rhino prefers to drink daily but can live up to five days without water.

Communication

Black rhinos use a range of vocalisations to communicate with their offspring, with other rhinos and when threatened. They may grunt, growl, scream, squeal, snort or trumpet. Bodily postures and scent markings are also used.

Reproduction

Black rhinos are polygamous and breed throughout the year. The majority of births take place at the end of the rainy season. The gestation period is between 419 and 478 days. The courtship can be complex and prolonged. To attract the female (cow), the male (bull) snorts, swings his head from side to side and then sweeps his horn across the ground. The mating pair may stay together for several weeks and mate several times a day. The female gives birth to a single calf. Weaning begins at two months and is complete by twelve months. The calf of a black rhino always walks behind its mother, and will remain with its mother for two to four years or until another calf is born. It is then chased away by its mother, to lead an independent life in solitude.

Females reach sexual maturity between five and seven years old and males between seven and nine years old.

Predators/Threats

Black rhinos have no natural predator apart from poachers who illegally hunt them for their horns. They are easy prey as they are creatures of habit living in a clearly defined home range. Their poor eyesight will not detect the presence of poachers until it is too late. Their horns are worth thousands of US dollars and are used in traditional Chinese medicine and as ceremonial daggers. The only other threat to the black rhino is loss of habitat.

Black & White Rhino Trivia

♦Black rhinos are nicknamed the hooked-lipped rhinoceros. White rhinos are nicknamed the square-lipped rhinoceros.

♦The black rhino is able to eat plants that are highly toxic to other animals, e.g. euphorbia.

♦The rhino belongs to the same family as the horse.

♦Removal of the rhinos' horns deters poachers. The rhinos are able to get along well without their horns, but the long term effect is unknown. The horns grow back at the rate of several inches a year.

♦Even when asleep the rhino is able to move its ears around to detect any noise.

♦The rhino may eat its own dung and this is believed to be a form of hormone replacement therapy.

♦The rhino holds its tail erect when running.

Cheetah
(Acinonyx jubatus)
Swahili: *Duma/Chita*

Identification
The cheetah is renowned as the world's fastest land animal. Its super light, flexible, streamlined body is lean and muscular in appearance. Its legs are long and thin.

The short, coarse fur is tan in colour and is covered with small round/oval black spots, which act as camouflage. The throat and underside are white.

The tail has spots, four to six dark rings and a white, bushy tuft at the tip.

The blunt, semi-retractable claws of the cheetah are visible and exert a traction effect when running at speed. The dew claw is short and sharp and is used to pull prey to the ground.

The brown eyes are set high, on a small head. Black teardrop-like marks, which absorb bright light and reduce the glare from the sun, run from the inner corner of each eye to the corner of the mouth. The backs of the ears, lips and nose are black.

The cheetah has excellent eyesight and sense of smell.

The male cheetah is slightly bigger than the female.

Head & Body Length:	1.2-1.4m
Tail Length:	0.6-0.8m
Shoulder Height:	70-90cm
Weight:	35-65kg

Life Span
Twelve years in the wild.

Habitat
Cheetahs are usually found in the savannahs, grasslands, deserts and open woodlands, in the vicinity of abundant plain grazers. Cheetahs are highly visible on the savannahs and need bushes and tall grasses to hide from the ever-present, marauding predators who stalk them.

34

Behaviour

Cheetahs are shy, solitary elusive animals.

Females remain solitary for life, unless they are raising cubs or there is a temporary mother-daughter allegiance.

Male cheetahs either live alone, which is rare, or in small groups known as a *coalition* of up to four males, which can last a lifetime. Males living in a coalition are very territorial and will kill intruders if necessary. They all contribute to marking their territory, by urinating, spraying urine, defecating and sharpening their claws on trees.

Cheetahs usually hunt on their own, and they prey on small antelopes. The cheetah has remarkable vision and can spot prey 5km away. However when a coalition hunts together, they are able to target larger prey such as wildebeest and zebra.

In order to be successful when stalking prey, the cheetah needs to get within 30-60m, before giving chase. They can achieve and maintain a top speed of 100km/h for 300m, if they are not successful within one minute they have to quit the chase, because of the sharp rise in body temperature and ensuing exhaustion. The increase in body temperature, if it is maintained, can lead to dehydration and brain damage. The cheetah's tail is used as a rudder when in pursuit, allowing it to manoeuvre sharply in response to its prey's constant change in direction. The cheetah uses its forefeet to trip its prey up, it then locks its jaws firmly onto the throat. The victim's death is by strangulation and is usually prolonged. Cheetahs are only about 50% successful when hunting prey.

The cheetah has to consume its prey quickly as the ever-present scavengers (lions, hyenas, jackals, leopards, and vultures) will move in quickly and relieve it of its catch. They only eat live prey, and do not cache food or return to a kill. Cheetahs are diurnal and hunt either early morning or late afternoon, resting at midday.

Diet

The cheetah is carnivorous, and hunts and kills small-to-medium-sized antelopes (oribi, springbok, gazelles), small mammals (hares) and game birds. It will hunt and kill larger antelopes (zebras, wildebeest) when hunting as a group.

The cheetah can go up to ten days without water.

Communication

Scent marking is the primary form of communication. Cheetahs use a wide variety of vocalisations to communicate with their offspring (chirping), with other cheetahs, or when threatened (growling). Visual signals, bodily postures, tactile/sociable greetings (sniffing, face licking and face/cheek rubbing) and antagonistic, aggressive behaviours are also used.

Reproduction

There is no distinct breeding season. Males are only found in the presence of females when mating. The gestation period is up to 98 days. The female can give birth to up to nine cubs, and she raises them on her own. Newborn cubs are blind and helpless, and their eyes open between 4-10 days. The  cubs initially have blue-grey fur with a black underside that quickly fades and takes on the colouration and markings of the adult. A fluffy grey *"mantle"* of hair runs from the neck down to the mid back. This begins to disappear at three months

The cubs are hidden in dense vegetation and rocks for the first month. They move from den to den every few days. Cubs are prey to hyenas, leopards, eagles and lions and the mortality rate is as high as 90%. Lions are four times the size of a cheetah and once the cubs have been discovered the female is unable to protect them

Cubs venture out with their mother at five to six weeks to join her for a kill, and they are weaned by three months.

The cubs have a long period of dependency, and this can be up to 24 months. Instinctively cheetahs do not know how to hunt, catch and kill prey and avoid predators, this must be taught by their mother. Before they are six months old the mother will bring home small, disabled, live prey for the cubs to practise chasing and killing under her supervision. They are unable to successfully kill on their own until they are 15 months old.

Cheetahs reach sexual maturity at two years old.

Predators/Threats

Cheetahs are illegally hunted by poachers for their fur and killed by locals when their livestock are threatened. Loss of habitat, competition from other predators for prey, and inbreeding (leading to congenital genetic type disorders) are the main threat to the cheetah's survival.

Trivia

◆*Cheetah* is a Hindu word that means "spotted one".

◆Cheetahs in the wild are prone to corneal injuries as they hunt with their eyes open and injure themselves by running into sharp thorns.

◆Cheetah flies, which are unique to cheetahs, are a nuisance and cause them tremendous irritation when present in large numbers.

◆Cheetahs are less aggressive than the other big cats and can be tamed.

◆Cheetahs can purr but cannot roar like a lion

◆Cheetah cubs that are brought up in captivity with only human contact are difficult or impossible to integrate back into the wild, as they have not been taught the art of hunting or survival by their mother.

◆Cheetahs in captivity are prone to gastritis and this is believed to be stress related.

Common Plains Zebra/Burchell's Zebra
(*Equus quagga* formerly *Equus burchelli*)
Swahili: *Punda milia*

Identification
Although generally recognised as being similar in appearance to a horse, the zebra has a short, stocky body and short legs.

Its most distinguishing feature is the coat: the zebra has broad, black and white stripes which are as individual as a human finger print.

The stripes are vertical over the head, neck, forequarters and body, but become horizontal towards the hindquarters. The stripes on the legs are narrow and horizontal and extend as far as the odd-toed black hooves.

The black and white striped, bristly mane is short and upright.

The tail is long, with a straggly dark tuft at the tip.

The zebra has large eyes on the side of the head, and has excellent peripheral vision. The ears are large and turn in all directions. The muzzle is black.

The zebra has excellent eyesight, hearing, sense of smell and taste.

Head & Body Length:	2-2.5m
Shoulder Height:	1-1.5m
Tail Length:	47-56cm
Weight:	175-385kg

Life Span
Twelve years in the wild.

Habitat
Zebras are found in the savannahs, grasslands and woodlands, up to altitudes of 4,500m.

Behaviour
Zebras are sociable animals, and live together in a harem. The harem is a stable, family group that is led and defended by one male (stallion), and has up to six females (mares) and their offspring. Occasionally, harems may come together, as in migration, to form a large herd.

A dominance hierarchy exists amongst the females. The dominant female who is the alpha female, leads the group and is the first one to mate with the male. The most recently acquired female is ranked the lowest.

A harem is created by a male abducting the fillies as they approach their first oestrus. If the male is successful, the filly will remain with him for the rest of her natural life. The male defends the harem vigorously from other predatory males and can hold a harem for up to 15 years.

Males leave the harem between the ages of one and four years old as a result of the arrival of new offspring and the continuing, deteriorating relationships that it has with its mother. Males may choose to live alone or with other males until they are able to have their own harem, which occurs at the age of six years old. Up until that age they do not have the necessary skills to manage and defend a harem.

Zebras are nomadic by nature and migrate with other species (wildebeest, gazelles) following the rains. They are the first grazer to enter the newly replenished grasslands. They graze on and trample the long grasses, leaving in their wake the succulent short grasses for the wildebeest and gazelles to feed on.

When threatened by predators, zebras unite in a tightly knit group that is virtually impregnable. For that reason alone, hyenas have a preference for hunting zebras in a pack. Zebras are able to run in short bursts at speeds of 65km/h to escape from predators.

Zebras sleep standing up and retreat to the plains at nighttime where there is good visibility. There are usually one or more lookouts throughout the night, spotting predators. The zebra's night vision is excellent.

Zebras are diurnal and nocturnal.

Diet
The zebra is a nomadic herbivore, spending the majority of its time grazing on long and short grasses. It will also browse on young shoots, herbs, leaves, shrubs, twigs and leaves. The digestive system has developed to allow the zebra to rapidly extract protein from food of poor nutritional value.

Because the zebra is able to eat short coarse grass, it cannot survive for long without water and is therefore usually found in close proximity to water sources.

Communication
The zebra's primary form of communication with each other is barking and whinnying. The position their ears assume is also a form of communication and is an indication of their mood, whether they are calm, frightened or angry. Zebras will use their lips and teeth to groom each other.

Reproduction
There is no distinct breeding season, but the peak season for giving birth is in the short dry season between December and January. Zebras are polygamous.

The gestation period is up to 365 days. The female gives birth to a single foal which is striped brown and white. Within 15 minutes of being born the foal is able to suckle, stand upright and walk. For a period of three days after the birth, until the foal is able to recognise its mother's voice, smell and sight, it is kept away from the harem. The foal is suckled for six months.

Fifty per cent of foals born are lost to predation. If threatened, the harem physically closes ranks, with the foal protected in the centre. The harem is aggressively defended by the male.

Zebras reach sexual maturity at three years old.

Predators/Threats
Zebras are very common and not an endangered species. They are hunted for their meat and hide and are natural prey for lions, hyenas, African wild dogs, cheetahs and leopards. Loss of habitat and lack of availability and access to water also threaten the zebra's survival.

Trivia

♦Burchell's zebras are named after the famous British explorer, William John Burchell.

♦Zebra is a Portuguese word that means "wild ass".

♦Zebras are closely related to donkeys and horses and can walk, trot, canter and gallop.

♦An upright mane is clear indication of good health in a zebra. A flagging mane is an indication of bad health. This is a result of loss of fat in the neck which supports the mane.

♦Burchell's zebras can mate with donkeys to produce a zebdonk, zonkey, zebrass or zorse.

♦Zebras are unpredictable by nature and this makes it difficult to domesticate them.

♦It is believed that the zebra's stripes act as camouflage when they are near long grasses, and that the stripes make it difficult for predators to differentiate one to the other when they are grouped together, especially in fading light.

Giraffe
(Giraffa camelopardalis)
Swahili: *Twiga*

Identification
The giraffe is a peaceful, cloven-hoofed ungulate and is the tallest mammal and largest ruminant in the world.

The background colour of the short fur is cream to tan, and is covered with an array of spots (polygons) in varying shades of brown that cover the entire body, apart from the underside. The spots darken with age.

The head of the giraffe is relatively small. It has large eyes with long lashes and medium-sized ears. The bump between the eyes (central swelling) is larger in the male. The muzzle is long and narrow. The prehensile, black tongue is up to 45cm long. It is toughened to enable the giraffe to eat the foliage of the acacia tree, including the thorns that are pulverised by the molars. The tongue is very effective at removing any insects on the face.

Both sexes have two horns (ossicones), which are up to13cm long. The female horns are smaller, and have tufts of black hair on them. The male horns tend to be bald due to the tufts of hair being removed with time as a result of regular necking and combat fights with other males. The male giraffe may develop an additional three horns that are formed from calcium deposits as a result of combat fights.

The neck is long, and consists of seven cervical vertebrae. The brown mane, which runs the length of the cervical spine, is short and upright. The back slopes sharply from the shoulders to the hind quarters.

The legs are long and thin, with the forelegs approximately 10% longer than the hind legs. When strolling along, the foreleg and hind leg of one side move forward together, and alternate with the opposite side. This results in a peculiar, ungainly gait which is not particularly noticeable when walking slowly. When running, both of the hind legs move forwards together and cross over on the outside of the forelegs. The giraffe can run at speeds of 56km/h over short distances.

The tail has a tassel of long black hair at the tip.

The giraffe has good eyesight.

Height: Male 4.7-6.2m
Female 3.9-5m
Tail Length: 0.8-1m
Weight: Male 1,100-1,900kg
Female 700-1,200kg
(These figures are dependent upon species).

Life Span
Twenty-five years in the wild.

Physiology
The sheer height and size of the giraffe requires a large heart that is capable of maintaining adequate blood pressure to the brain. A combination of a series of one-way valves situated in the neck, and a network of finely meshed, elasticated veins and arteries at the base of the brain, prevents pooling of blood in the brain when the giraffe lowers its head to drink and reduces the pressure when it lifts its head up quickly. The body weight places additional pressure on the blood vessels in the lower legs. Toughened skin and an extra-tight sheath encapsulate the legs and maintain adequate pressure and circulation.

Habitat
Giraffes are found in the savannahs, open plains, grasslands, woodlands, and dense forests, particularly in the vicinity of the acacia tree.

Behaviour
Giraffes are non territorial, sociable animals, living in a leaderless, disorganised group, called a herd, of up to 20 individuals. Giraffes do not establish long-term relationships therefore membership of the herd is fluid and constantly changes.

43

The herd includes females (cows), their offspring and younger males. Females usually stay with a herd. Dominance among the males (bulls) in the herd is established by necking. Males may live together in bachelor herds, while older males live a solitary life in isolation.

The giraffe sleeps standing up, for a period of up two hours per day. They may occasionally rest on the ground with their legs folded beneath them, this makes them vulnerable to their predators as they have difficulty rising from the ground quickly.

Giraffes are diurnal and nocturnal.

Diet

The giraffe is a herbivore and browser and spends up to 20 hours a day eating. They browse on bark, twigs, leaves, fruit, flowers, seed pods, climbers, vines and herbs. They have a particular liking for the foliage of the mimosa and acacia tree.

The giraffe is able to survive on very little water. When water is available they drink copious amounts, and in order to do so they have to splay their forelegs wide apart so they can lower their head and neck. In doing so they put themselves at risk from their predators.

Communication

Giraffes are quiet animals. They communicate infrasonically, but will use a variety of sounds to communicate with each other when required—grunting, snorting, hissing, whistling and coughing.

Reproduction

Giraffes are polygamous and breed throughout the year. The majority of the births take place in the dry months.

The males are constantly searching for females that are in oestrus, and detect this by smelling and tasting the female's urine.

The gestation period is up to 465 days. The female gives birth to a single calf while standing up. The calf, which is usually 1.8m tall, is able to run around shortly after being born. For the first two weeks of its life the calf spends a lot of its time lying down and resting. It is particularly vulnerable to predators such as lions, hyenas, leopards and wild dogs. Only 25-50% of calves reach adulthood.

While being fed by its mother the calf will be placed in a crèche alongside other calves, allowing its mother to go in search of food. The females take it in turn to look after the young calves. The calves grow at the rate of 2.5cm per day.

By the time the calf is six months old, it is relatively independent of its mother. Full independence is achieved between the ages of one and three years old.

Females reach sexual maturity between the ages of three to four years old. Males reach sexual maturity between the ages of four to five years old but do not breed until they are eight years old.

Predators/Threats

Although lions are the only predator to threaten the adult giraffe, they are hunted by humans for their meat, hide and hair. However the main threat to the giraffe's survival is loss of habitat.

Trivia

♦Giraffe is an Arabic word that means "one that walks very fast". It can cover 4.5m with a single stride.

♦Giraffes were nicknamed "camelopards" by the ancient Romans, who believed that they resembled a cross between a camel and a leopard.

♦Necking is used in combat but can also be a sign of affection.

♦Giraffes are plagued by ticks, which are effectively removed by the oxpecker bird.

♦Giraffes are not a threat to humans or their livestock because they are a browser, eating foliage at a high level.

♦The female giraffe can delay the birth of the calf by up to two months until climatic and environmental conditions are more favourable.

♦The giraffe is the only animal to be born with horns (ossicones).

♦When threatened, the giraffe can deliver a single powerful blow with its legs that is capable of killing a man or lion instantly.

♦Some African tribes treat nose bleeds by using smoke from the burning hide of a giraffe.

♦The meat of a giraffe is edible and tastes like camel.

♦Local inhabitants openly try to sell tourists bracelets made from the tail hair of the giraffe.

♦Adult male giraffes develop glands underneath the skin that release an offensive rancid odour. Bull giraffes are nicknamed stink bulls.

Red-Billed Oxpecker Bird
(*Buphagus erythrorhynchus*)
Swahili: *Askari wa kiaru*

The red billed oxpecker bird or "tick bird" has a symbiotic relationship with its host and is regularly spotted riding round on the backs of antelope, eland, rhinos, hippos, giraffes, impala, zebras, warthogs and buffaloes, to name but a few.

It is semi-parasitic, living on a diet of dead skin, scabs, crabs, open wounds, ticks, larvae, fleas and flies from its host. It has a shrill, raucous alarm call that alerts its host and those nearby to the presence of predators.

The oxpecker bird is usually found in savannahs, bushlands, grasslands and wooded forest areas, being particularly common in national parks and game reserves.

Ruminants

Ruminants have a three-to-four-chambered stomach that allows them to process indigestible plant material into food of nutritional value. The half-chewed food is swallowed and enters the *rumen*, which is the first chamber of the stomach. This partly digested food is later regurgitated for further chewing and is known as *cud*. This process is repeated many times before the food continues through and exits the digestive system.

Trivia
♦Ruminants produce copious amounts of gas.
♦Ruminants' dung is fine ground.

Ticks
Swahili: *Kupe*

Ticks are small, blood-sucking, parasitic mites that live on mammals (including humans), birds and reptiles. They are capable of passing on dangerous, life-threatening diseases.

The tick bites the host, and inserts a probe into the skin. Having attached itself firmly, it slowly begins sucking blood. They are very difficult for the host to remove, and this is usually done by an oxpecker bird or by the host wallowing in mud. When submerged in clear water an air bubble forms around the tick's mouth, providing it with oxygen, but if thick mud is present, the small air bubbles cannot form, so the tick is deprived of oxygen and dies. Afterwards the host rubs itself against a tree or rock to remove the mud and the tick.

Hippopotamus
(*Hippopotamus amphibius*)
Swahili: *Kiboko*

Identification

The hippopotamus is the third largest mammal in the world.

The hippo's thick, smooth, sensitive skin is brown to greyish purple in colour, but the creases and the underside are pink. It has no sweat glands, but the pores secrete a colourless, oily substance, (blood sweat), which turns red and eventually brown. This acts as a moisturiser, sunscreen and anti-bacterial agent. Hair is present as bristles around the nose, mouth, ears and on the tip of the short, paddle-like tail. There is a sparse covering of fine hair over the whole body.

The hippo has a large, barrel-shaped body. Its legs are short and stumpy. There are four webbed toes on each foot that help to support and distribute its weight when it is on land.

The hippo has a large, broad head. The mouth is enormous with long, sharp, tusk-like canine teeth that may be up to 72cm long. The mouth opens to an angle of 150°.

The eyes and ears are small and are placed high on the head, allowing it to almost completely submerge. They have excellent eyesight and hearing, and a keen sense of smell.

Head & Body Length:	3.3-4.6m
Shoulder Height:	1.5-1.6m
Tail Length:	35-50cm
Weight:	1,800-3,600kg

Life Span

Forty-five years in the wild.

Habitat

Hippos are found resting and wallowing in wetlands, freshwater lakes, dams, slow-flowing rivers and swamps during the day, and at night they forage in the surrounding grasslands.

Behaviour

Hippos either live on their own, or in a family group called a pod. The average pod size is 15 but can be as big as 30. The pod includes the dominant territorial male (bull), females (cow), their offspring and inferior, submissive males. The only social bond is between the female and the calf.

Hippos have a sedentary lifestyle, resting, sleeping and wallowing in mud or water for up to 16 hours a day. The water keeps the hippo cool, and prevents the skin from cracking, drying out and getting sunburnt. The eyes, ears and nostrils close when the hippo dives underwater. The hippo is able to submerge and resurface by inflating or deflating the lungs, and is able to remain under water for six minutes. They defecate in large quantities while in the water.

Male hippos are fiercely aggressive and territorial in water and will not tolerate the presence of another male. Only submissive males that have no mating rights are tolerated in the pod. Territories cover up to 250m along the bank of the river side. They mark their territory by urinating backwards and spreading dung, as they defecate, with their swirling, short, paddle-like tail.

Hippos are not territorial on land, and emerge from the water on an evening to forage on their own. Travelling a well worn path of up to 10km, they spend four to five hours searching for food, consuming up to 45kg of grass. The hippo returns to the water before dawn.

Despite its cumbersome appearance the hippo is surprisingly graceful in water, and on land it is able to run at speeds of 40km/h over a short distance.

Hippos are diurnal and nocturnal.

Diet

The hippo is a herbivore and grazer, feeding on aquatic plants during the day, emerging from the water in the evening to feed on grass, crops, leaves, roots, tubers and wood bark in the surrounding grasslands. The hippo is reputed to have carnivorous tendencies and may eat carrion or small mammals if the opportunity arises.

Communication
Hippos use a variety of vocalisations to communicate with each other in and out of the water—honking, wheezing, grunting and bellowing. Constant yawning is a warning sign.

Reproduction
Hippos are polygamous and breed throughout the year. The majority of births take place in the rainy season, when food is plentiful. The gestation period is up to 240 days. The female withdraws from the pod for a period of 14 days and gives birth to a single calf, this can occur either on land or in the water. The female is highly protective of its young calf. The calf is able to suckle under water. Weaning occurs between six and eight months. The calf remains with its mother until the next calf is born.

Females reach sexual maturity between five and six years old. Males reach sexual maturity between seven and eight years old.

Predators/Threats
The hippo has no natural predators, apart from poachers who illegally hunt them for their meat, hide and ivory canine teeth. Lions, crocodiles and hyenas are the main threat to the calf. Loss of habitat is the only other threat to the hippos' survival.

Trivia
♦The word hippopotamus comes from a Greek word meaning "river horse".

♦The hippo is Africa's most aggressive and dangerous animal and is responsible for more human deaths than any other animal. Humans are often killed by their boats being capsized, and then being drowned or bitten severely, but they can also be killed by being trampled on or bitten when the hippos are out foraging at night.

♦Male hippos are easy to sex, as they are covered in scars as a result of combat fights with other males.

♦It is a myth that hippos can swim, they propel their bodies along the bottom of the river/pool bed with their legs.

♦Hippos dehydrate faster than any other mammal and need water deep enough to submerge in to keep cool.

Leopard
(*Panthera pardus*)
Swahili: *Chui*

Identification
The leopard is the smallest of the four big cats (tiger, lion, jaguar and leopard).

It has a long body and tail, with short, powerful legs. The broad paws have long, hooked, retractable claws that enable the leopard to climb trees.

The soft, dense, tawny-tan fur is covered with black circular rosettes. The underside is lighter with black spots. Single black spots are present on the head, throat, chest, and lower limbs. White spots are found behind the ears and on the tip of the tail.

The leopard's head is large in comparison with the rest of its body. The jaws are strong and powerful. It has small, rounded ears and yellow eyes with circular pupils.

The leopard has good eyesight, excellent hearing and a keen sense of smell.

Head & Body Length:	90cm-1.7m
Shoulder Height:	45-80cm
Tail Length:	60cm-1m
Weight:	30-90kg

Life Span
Fifteen years in the wild.

Habitat
Leopards are adaptable and are the most widely distributed of the big cats. They are found in savannahs, grasslands, desert plains, woodlands, forests and mountainous regions.

Behaviour
Secretive, solitary and elusive, the leopard is extremely difficult to spot in the wild, spending the daylight hours resting high in the trees. It hunts alone, during the hours of darkness between dusk and dawn. By nature, the leopard is extremely dangerous, aggressive and unpredictable.

Leopards are highly territorial and regularly patrol and defend their home range. They mark the boundaries of their territory with urine, faeces and claw marks on trees.

The leopard is a highly skilled and accomplished predator, using stealth and cunning to get close to the prey. They are extremely quick and agile and can run at speeds of 60km/h and are capable of bringing down prey three times their size. Giving chase over a short distance they pounce on their prey, and deliver a swift, powerful bite to the throat, that kills instantly. Leopards are known to kill prey when they are not hungry and will cache it away, either up a tree or in dense vegetation, away from other predators and scavengers such as hyenas and lions. They can return several days later to feed on the decomposing flesh.

Leopards are nocturnal.

Diet
The leopard is carnivorous and a highly efficient killer. It hunts and kills small to medium ungulates (antelope, gazelles), small mammals, primates, rodents, birds, fish and reptiles. It also preys on cheetah cubs.
Leopards can survive long periods without water.

Communication
Leopards are solitary animals and use scent marking and claw marking to make their presence known. A variety of vocalisations — growling, roaring, hissing, grunting and meowing, are utilised to communicate their mood and presence.

Reproduction
Leopards are polygamous and breed throughout the year. Solitary males are found in the company of a female (leopardess) for a period of one week, when they are in oestrous. There may on occasions be a fight for reproductive rights if another male is present.

Courtship is a tense and noisy affair, with the female presenting herself in a crouched position. They mate continuously.

The gestation period is up to 105 days. The female gives birth to two to four cubs in a secluded spot, surrounded by dense vegetation and boulders. The cubs are hidden for up to eight weeks. They open their eyes after ten days. Their coat is a smoky grey colour, and has faded, poorly defined rosettes.

The female has a strong maternal bond with her cubs and raises them on her own. The cubs are suckled for three months and begin to eat meat at six to seven weeks. Instinctively leopards do not know how to hunt, catch and kill prey and survive as a predator, this must taught by their mother. The cubs accompany their mother on hunts at three months old. Small, disabled, live prey is used by the mother to teach the cubs the art of hunting, chasing and finally killing. By 12 months old the cubs are able to fend for themselves but may remain with their mother for up to 18-24 months.

Leopards are sexually mature between two to three years old.

Predators/Threats
Leopards are hunted by poachers for their fur and are killed by locals when their livestock are threatened. Loss of habitat, especially trees, and competition from other predators for prey are the main threat to the leopard's survival.

Trivia
♦Leopards are the largest spotted cat.

♦Leopards are the most elusive of the big cats, due partly to the fact that they are nocturnal and spend the daylight hours resting high up in a tree.

♦If a leopard is habituated it loses its natural fear and respect for humans, and can never be returned to the wild because of the danger it poses to tourists and local inhabitants.

♦Leopards like water and are good swimmers.

♦Black leopards are known as panthers.

♦Leopards are poached for their whiskers as well as their hide.

♦Leopards are the most adept of all the big cats at climbing trees

Lion
(Panthera leo)
Swahili: *Simba*

Identification

Lions have large, powerful, muscular bodies and are the second largest member of the cat family, after tigers.

The short, coarse fur is a uniformly coloured golden yellow. The underside is lighter in colour.

The head is rounded, and the jaw strong, with long, powerful canine teeth. The amber eyes are spread wide. Excellent eyesight, good hearing and a keen sense of smell make lions a formidable predator.

Quick reflexes, combined with strong hind legs, enable the lion to pounce on its prey. The forelegs are more suited to grasping and knocking down prey, and are assisted by claws that are retractable and razor sharp.

The male's thick, shaggy mane covers the ears, neck and shoulders. The colour of the mane ranges from blonde to black, and darkens with age. The mane makes the male lion more attractive to females and offers some degree of protection to vital structures around the head and neck when fighting.

Both male and female lions have a distinctive black tuft of hair on the tip of the tail. This develops at five months onwards.

Males are up to 50% heavier than females.

Head & Body Length:	Male 1.7-2.5m
	Female 1.4-1.75m
Shoulder Height:	Male 1.2m
	Female 1m
Tail Length:	0.7-1m
Weight:	Male 150-240kg
	Female 120-180kg

Life Span

Sixteen years in the wild. Females live longer and are more numerous than male lions. The majority of males do not live beyond ten years, and usually die a violent death. Their risky lifestyle involves them engaging in frequent bouts of fighting with other males for dominance of the pride.

Habitat

Lions are usually found in savannahs, grasslands, bushlands, woodlands and semi-deserts.

Behaviour

The lion is a sociable animal, living and hunting together in a permanent group called a pride. The average size of a pride is 15 but they can be as big as 30.

The pride consists of 4-12 related females (lionesses) who remain with the pride for life, as well as offspring, and a small number of unrelated adult males known as a coalition, who mate with and defend the females.

Male lions can lead a pride for up to three years. However the average length of time is 18 months.

Lions are territorial and regularly patrol their boundaries at night, marking the territory with urine, faeces or scent from their paws.

Lions tend to hunt under the cover of darkness, but are particularly active at dusk and at sunrise. Male lions do not usually participate in hunting, unless they are nomadic.

The lionesses work together as a highly organised, coordinated and successful team, in difficult, open terrain. Females are more suited to hunting than males, as they are smaller, more agile and less conspicuous. When hunting, they outmanoeuvre the prey by identifying, isolating and encircling the victim, usually getting to within 30m before launching a swift strike. They are able to run at speeds of 48-59km/h for only a few seconds. The endurance of their prey tends to be much better — zebras and gazelles can accelerate and outrun a lion in less than six seconds. The victim is either strangled with a crushing bite to the windpipe, or is suffocated by the jaws completely encasing its muzzle. This 'kiss of death' is usually quick and clean. On very rare occasions the victim may be eaten alive.

After a kill the male eats first, followed by the lionesses and then the cubs. The feasting goes on for hours. The remains of the kill are left to scavengers.

Where adult male lions are present at a kill it is rare for the pride to be bothered by hyenas.

Where there are fewer than five females present, hyenas are usually successful at stealing the kill.

Lions are nocturnal.

Diet

The lion is carnivorous and is a highly efficient killer. Being at the top of the food chain, it has little to fear. Its skill, speed and strength allows it to successfully hunt and kill animals three times its size.

The lion hunts and kills medium to large ungulates (wildebeest, zebras), other predators and their cubs (leopards and cheetahs in particular), small mammals, rodents, birds and reptiles. It is not unknown for a lion to scavenge from other predators, hyenas in particular.

It is extremely rare for a lion to attack a buffalo or giraffe because of risk of serious injury to itself.

Lions can survive long periods without water.

Communication

Lions are unusual among the cats as they are sociable and live together in a commune. They spend up to 20 hours a day resting and sleeping in the shade. They display affection towards each other with facial and bodily postures and tactile behaviours that involve touching, rubbing and licking the head and neck. They use a variety of vocalisations to communicate with each other, purring to display pleasure, and roaring as a means to locate each other, to establish territory and to advertise their presence.

Reproduction

There is no distinct breeding season. The male members of the pride do not have established mating rights. The first male to encounter a female in oestrus has the rights.

It is usual for the females to give birth at approximately the same time as each other. This increases the cubs' chances of survival as they all develop at the

same rate. The females share the responsibility of rearing the cubs together.

The gestation period is up to 120 days. The female gives birth to up to six cubs in a secluded spot away from the pride. Newborn cubs are blind, with their eyes opening after one week. They have lightly coloured brown spots on their bodies that fade away with time. The cubs are introduced to the pride after a period of six to eight weeks. Weaning occurs between six to seven months. They begin to participate in hunting at one year old and are able to hunt effectively by two, at which stage they usually leave their mother.

When young males reach maturity, they either leave the pride voluntarily or are forced to leave. Remaining is not an option, as they are systematically killed. They then lead a nomadic life, either on their own or with another male, until they are five years old and are able to challenge and take over their own pride. They have fully developed manes by the age of four years old. Young lions have pink noses until they are about four years old after that black pigment begins to cover the nose.

The mortality rate for cubs is high, at about 80%. They are easy prey for jackals, hyenas, leopards, vultures, snakes and the occasional nomadic male lion. Death by starvation is common among cubs. They are last in the pecking order at a kill, and by the time their turn comes round, there is very little meat left. New males that challenge and take over a pride will kill all of the cubs that they encounter. This brings the females into oestrus, so that he can then father the next set of cubs in the pride.

Females reach sexual maturity at four years old. Males reach sexual maturity between three and five years old.

Predators/Threats

There are only 25,000 lions left in Africa. In the last decade the lion population has declined between 20-50%. Lions are illegally hunted by poachers and killed by locals when their

livestock are threatened. Loss of habitat, competition from other predators for prey, inbreeding and exposure to viruses are also threats to the lion's survival. Disease spreads easily amongst lions because they are sociable and a pride can soon be decimated. The effects of climate change should not be underestimated, the resulting drought and floods provide perfect conditions for the spread of epidemic diseases.

Trivia

♦The lion's mane is a strong indicator of its health and fitness: the darker and the thicker the mane, the healthier the lion. A lion with a black mane is superior, has more testosterone, will live longer and is more likely to survive from being wounded.

♦A lion's roar can be heard up to 8km away.

♦If a lion is habituated it loses its natural fear and respect of humans, and can never return to the wild because of the danger it poses to tourists and local inhabitants.

♦When stalking prey, the lion may wait up to nine hours before launching an attack.

♦Lions are not very efficient at losing heat, and this causes them to be quite lethargic during the day.

♦Lions' tongues are extremely abrasive—a triangular pattern of barbs that point backwards towards the throat to help strip skin and flesh from the bones of their prey.

♦A lion's night time vision is six times more powerful than a human's.

♦Small antelopes, such as the dik dik or impala, are captured alive by adult lions and are used as bait to teach the cubs the art of successful hunting.

♦Lone, male lions are particularly dangerous. They have usually been cast out of the pride by younger males who are competing for dominance. Being old, weak and injured and having no females to hunt for them, they turn to hunting for the weakest of prey, and that may include humans.

Spotted Hyena
(Crocuta crocuta)
Swahili: *Fisi*

Identification

The hyena has a dog-like appearance.

Its most recognisable feature is a sloping back — this is due to the forelegs being longer and more muscular than the hind legs. There are four claws on each foot that are non-retractable and blunt.

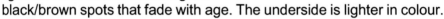

The short, rough fur is tan to light brown in colour with irregular black/brown spots that fade with age. The underside is lighter in colour.

The mane is coarse and has reversed fur (fur that lies in an upward direction towards the head).

The tail is short and bushy with a black tuft at the end and hangs down when standing or walking.

The head of the hyena is small in comparison to the size of its body. It has large rounded ears, a dark muzzle and a black nose.

The genitals of the female resemble those of the male, which makes it very difficult to distinguish between the sexes.

Body Length: 0.95-1.5m
Shoulder Height: 75-85cm
Tail Length: 25-35cm
Weight: Male 56-63kg Female 67-75kg

Life Span
Twelve years in the wild.

Habitat
Hyenas are usually found in savannahs and grasslands, although they can be found in woodlands, tropical rain forests, forest edges, and outskirts of the desert and in mountains up to 4,000m. They are able to survive near human habitations.

Behaviour
Hyenas live together in a clan, which is a permanent social group. The clans are hierarchical, complex and sociable. The average clan size is up to 12 hyenas, but can be as big as 90.

A single alpha female, the matriarch, dominates clan life. Male hyenas are subservient and dominated by the females, and in the hyena social hierarchy they are ranked the lowest. Males leave the clan when they reach sexual maturity and go in search of a new clan. Females remain with the clan for life.

Individually hyenas are not territorial, but once a group has been formed they will defend their territory aggressively. Clan life centres on the den, which is situated in the centre of the territory. The den has several entrances with numerous underground, interconnecting tunnels.

The hyenas mark the perimeter of their territory with a strong-smelling, yellow-coloured, oily substance that is excreted from the anal glands. Faeces deposited in latrines, and glands in their feet also allow them to scent-mark their territory.

Despite its reputation as an opportunistic scavenger, the hyena is actually a bold, dangerous, highly skilled and organised hunter.

Hyenas hunt on their own or in a small group. Hunting and tracking medium to larger ungulates is a team effort, initiated by one member of the pack. The hyena's keen hearing, eyesight and sense of smell is essential for hunting and their large heart gives them the ability to run long distances at 10km/h without tiring. They can achieve speeds of 60km/h over short distances when required.

Mainly nocturnal, hyenas are particularly active at dusk. In game reserves they tend to be diurnal, sleeping from 10 a.m. until 4 p.m. to avoid the oppressive heat.

Diet
The hyena is Africa's most common carnivore. Depending on what is available it will kill small (Grants gazelle) to large (buffalo) ungulates. The hyena's preference is for medium-sized ungulates. Its diet consists primarily of wildebeest, zebra and Thomson's gazelle, but it will eat birds, fish, tortoises, lizards, snakes, fruit, eggs, invertebrates, and other animals' excrement.

Hyenas raid food stores and crops close to human habitation.

A combination of powerful jaws and teeth and highly acidic fluids within its digestive tract enables the hyena to digest its entire prey. Hair, horns and hooves are later regurgitated in the form of pellets. The hyena's faeces is white due to the high calcium content; as such it is easily recognisable.

The hyena can consume up to 18kg of meat at one time, almost one third of its body weight. This raises the body temperature and the hyena needs to rest afterwards to cool down.

Communication

Hyenas are very vocal and use a wide range of vocalisations to communicate with each other—eleven in total. Hyenas also communicate by tactile phallic inspection, social grooming (mother and offspring only), scent-marking boundaries, and through body postures and courtship rituals.

Reproduction

There is no distinct breeding season. Hyenas are polygamous and to prevent in-breeding the females mate with males from other clans. Courtship can last for up to a year.

The gestation period is up to 110 days. The female gives birth to two to four cubs and raises them on her own. The cubs are black at birth. Born with their eyes open and with fully developed teeth, cubs of the same sex will either fight to the death or severely maim rival siblings until only one is able to survive. Cubs are introduced to the clan at two weeks old.

Cubs are suckled on milk for up to 18 months. The milk has an extremely high protein and fat content, which allows the female to go on long foraging trips leaving the cubs for periods of up to nine days without feeding them. Because of the speed at which hyenas eat, they are unable to regurgitate their food to feed their young.

The cubs remain in the den until 12 months old, after which they accompany their mothers on foraging trips. Young hyenas are dependent on the clan system for their survival until they are two to three years old.

Hyenas reach sexual maturity at about three years old.

Threats/Predators

Lions are the only predator to threaten the hyena. When livestock are threatened, humans actively hunt hyenas. However, the main threat to the hyena's survival is loss of habitat.

Trivia

♦The hyena is closely related to the cat and mongoose and is believed to be the evolutionary link between dogs and cats.

♦Female hyenas are 10% larger than the male and are more aggressive.

♦Male hyenas do not cock a leg to urinate.

♦Hyenas are very good swimmers.

♦Locals refer to the hyena as the dustbin man, as they rid the landscape of dead animal remains; they are also superstitious of hyenas and call them the dog of the devil.

♦Hyenas are known as Nandi witches. They travel on an evening from the Nandi forests to Nairobi carrying a torch made from bark and moss. It is believed that they engage in witchcraft and have to return to the forest by sunrise in animal form.

♦In captivity hyenas can become very tame.

♦Hyenas are not on the trophy hunters' hit list because they are deemed ugly and unattractive.

♦Traditionally the Maasai leave their dead on the plains for the hyena to consume.

White Rhinoceros
(*Ceratotherium simum*)
Swahili: *Faru/Kifaru*

Identification

The white rhino is one of the world's largest pure grazers, and the second largest mammal.

The white rhino's thick, smooth, hairless skin is grey, but can be varying shades of brown if it has been wallowing in mud. The skin harbours parasites such as ticks, fleas and crabs. It has no sweat glands. Hair is present on the fringes of the ears, on the tip of the short tail and as eyelashes.

The white rhino has a large, rotund body with a broad chest. A prominent hump straddles the base of the short neck and shoulders, this houses large powerful muscles and strong ligaments required to raise the head from the grazing position. Its legs are short and stumpy. It is an odd-toed ungulate having three toes on hooved feet. Its footprint resembles the ace of spades.

The head is large with an elongated face. It has a broad snout, large nostrils and a large square-shaped muzzle. Incisors and canine teeth are absent and it is heavily dependent on its muscular lips to grasp the short grass. Two horns made of keratin sit centrally behind the nose. The horns have no bony skeletal attachment but actually grow from the skin and continue to grow throughout life. The anterior horn is longer than the posterior horn.

The white rhino's keen sense of smell and hearing compensate for its poor eyesight. The eyes are very small and are placed on either side of the head. In order to look straight ahead the rhino has to turn its head sideways. The white rhino is short sighted and cannot detect an immobile object at 30m. They can detect a moving object at 30-50m. The large, prominent, funnel-shaped ears are mobile and move independently of each other.

Head & Body Length:	3.25-5m	
Shoulder Height:	1.5-1.9m	
Tail Length:	50-70cm	
Weight:	Male	1,800-2,500kg
	Female	1,800-2,000kg
Horn:	Anterior	90cm-1.5m
	Posterior	55cm

Combined Horn Weight: 6kg
Males are slightly heavier than females.

Life Span
Fifty years in the wild.

Habitat
White rhinos are found in open areas such as plains, savannahs and grasslands. They like to be near water holes, mud wallows and the shade of the trees.

Behaviour
Docile, sedentary, and sociable, the white rhino may be found in small stable groups of up to six called a "crash" or "herd". The crash is made up of females (cows), their offspring, the occasional male (bull) and sub adults. Crashes of ten rhinos are transient.

Female white rhinos are not territorial, and are tolerant of other white rhinos that encroach on their home range.

Adult male white rhinos live in solitary isolation, associating with females only when they are mating. They defend their territory aggressively and regularly patrol the boundaries. The perimeter is scent-marked at regular intervals with urine and dung heaps or middens. Urine is sprayed backwards by the male at great force in the direction of bushes and trees. Dung heaps are used by all passing rhinos.

The white rhino avoids conflict by moving away. When threatened it adopts an erect posture, lower its head and wipes its horn on the ground before charging. If a group of rhinos are threatened they form a formidable circle, with their rumps in the centre and their heads facing outwards. Despite its cumbersome appearance the white rhino can run at speeds of 40-50km/h in short bursts.

The white rhino is active early in the morning and in the evening. During the day it likes to rest and wallow in mud. The mud cools the white rhino down. Dried mud acts as a sun screen, exfoliator and helps to deter ticks, flies and other parasites.

The white rhino is both diurnal and nocturnal.

Diet
The white rhino is a herbivore and grazes heavily on grass and leaves, usually feeding and walking at the same time. It feeds early morning and evening and during the night.

The white rhino prefers to drink daily but can live up to five days without water.

Communication
White rhinos use a range of vocalisations to communicate with offspring, other rhinos and when threatened. They may grunt, growl, squeal, snort or trumpet. Bodily postures and scent marking are also utilised.

Reproduction
There is no distinct breeding season. White rhinos are polyandrous and polygamous. Male white rhinos only associate with females when mating. Courtships can last several days, and mating for up to one hour.

The gestation period is between 480-548 days. The female gives birth to a single calf in a secluded spot away from the crash. Within an hour of being born the calf is able to stand and suckle. Weaning begins at two months and is complete by twelve months. The calf of the white rhino always walks in front of its mother, and will remain with its mother for two to four years or until another calf is born. It is then chased way by its mother to lead an independent life in solitude.

Females reach sexual maturity between six and seven years old. Males reach sexual maturity between seven and eight years old.

Predators/Threats
No natural predators, apart from poachers who illegally hunt them for their horns. They are easy prey, as they are creatures of habit living in a clearly defined home range. Their poor eyesight will not detect the presence of poachers until is too late. Their horns are worth thousands of US dollars and are used in traditional Chinese medicine and as ceremonial daggers.

The only other threat to the white rhino is loss of habitat.

Black & White Rhino Trivia

♦Black rhinos are nicknamed the hooked-lipped rhinoceros. White rhinos are nicknamed the square-lipped rhinoceros.

♦The rhino belongs to the same family as the horse.

♦Removal of the rhinos' horns deters poachers. The rhinos are able to get along well without their horns, but the long term effect is unknown. The horns grow back at the rate of several inches a year. Even when asleep the rhino is able to move its ears around to detect any noise.

♦The rhino may eat its own dung, and this is believed to be a form of hormone replacement therapy.

♦The rhino holds its tail erect when running.

Differences Between a Black Rhino and a White Rhino

The white rhino is almost twice the size of the black rhino.

The black rhino has a longer neck than the white rhino as it has to reach up into trees and bushes to feed. The white rhino has a prominent hump that straddles the base of the neck and shoulders.

The black rhino has a prehensile, pointed hooked lip. The white rhino has a square-shaped muzzle.

The black rhino is commonly found in areas of thick vegetation. The white rhino is commonly found on the savannahs.

The black rhino is a browser — its natural head posture is held upwards towards the branches of the tree. The white rhino is a grazer — its natural head posture faces downwards towards the grass.

The black female rhino walks in front of her calf. The white female rhino walks behind her calf.

The black rhino is solitary. The white rhino is more sociable and is found in groups.

The black rhino is more aggressive than the white rhino, whereas the white rhino is quite docile.

White Rhino

Black Rhino

Antelope
Swahili: *Swala*

Fifty species of antelope can be found in the continents of Africa and Asia, inhabiting a variety of environments ranging from tropical forests, mixed forests, marshlands, grasslands and savannahs to deserts and mountainous areas.

Antelopes are elegant, agile, cloven-hoofed ungulates that vary in size, shape and colour. Their short fur is light brown to grey. Antelopes that live on the plains are particularly vulnerable to predation and usually have an array of blotches or stripes on their head, body and legs to act as camouflage. Some species have white makings on their rumps that act as a warning signal to others when they are on the run from predators. Their legs are long, slender and powerful.

Antelopes have large eyes with elongated horizontal pupils, and large ears. They have excellent eyesight, and a keen sense of smell and hearing.

Their horns are hollow and lightweight and usually last a lifetime.

The males (buck) are usually larger than the females (doe).

Antelopes are herbivores and ruminants, and are either a grazer or a browser or a combination of both. Antelopes that are pure grazers are water-dependent and need to drink every one to two days, whereas the browsers are able to extract sufficient moisture from the plants they feed on. All antelopes are diurnal, feeding early morning and late afternoon.

Antelopes that live in or near woodlands and forests where there is a constant, plentiful supply of food and water usually remain there throughout their natural lives. The antelopes on the plains are constantly on the move searching for food and water.

The majority of antelopes live in large herds on the open plains either in bachelor herds made up of young males, small herds of females, mixed herds or solitary bulls. Some species of antelope live on their own.

Most antelopes are polygamous, however a few species (dik-dik, klipspringer, blue duiker) are monogamous. The African antelope only produce one offspring. The gestation period for the small to medium-sized antelope is 120-182 days and for the larger antelope is 243-273 days.

Antelopes reproduce when there is an abundance of food, and in some cases are able to reproduce all year round.

Antelopes are prey for all the major predators, who seek out the young, sick, injured and old. They are one of the world's fastest land animals, and, being extremely agile, their constant dodging, twisting, turning and change of direction enables them to confuse and outrun most predators. Some species go into hiding in the bush when threatened.

Antelopes use a variety of vocalisations to communicate with each other. Visual signals, scent marking, tactile behaviours and bodily postures are also used. When threatened, intimidated or required to assert their dominance they will utilise antagonistic, aggressive behaviours.

When alarmed or excited antelopes are able to jump up and down on extended, straight legs. All four legs leave the ground at once and the back is arched — this is known as pronking or stotting. This demonstrates to any watching predators that they are fit and would not be easy prey. Glands in the hoofs release scent that allows any antelopes that have lost their way to find their way back to the herd.

Antelopes are natural prey for lions, leopards, cheetahs, African wild dogs, pythons and hyenas. They are hunted for their meat and hide. Loss of habitat is also a threat to their survival.

List of African Antelopes

Bongo, bushbuck, dik-dik, duiker, eland, gerenuk, gemsbok, Grant's gazelle, grysbok, hartebeest, impala, klipspringer, kob, kudu, nyala, oribi, oryx, reedbuck, roan antelope, sable antelope, saiga, sitatunga antelope, springbok, steinbok, suni, Thomson's gazelle, topi and waterbuck.

Common Eland
(*Taurotragus oryx*)
Swahili: *Mpofu/Mbungu/Pofu*

Identification

The eland is the largest and slowest species of antelope.

The eland is a large, muscular antelope with a cow-like resemblance. It has a smooth, light tan-coloured coat, with a blue-grey hue over the neck and shoulders that darkens with age. Males are darker than females. Narrow, vertical white stripes may be present over the forequarters.

The neck is short and thickened and a hump straddles the shoulders. A large, loose fold of skin covered in black hair, hangs down underneath the neck—this is known as the dewlap. The dewlap on the male is more prominent and increases in size with age.

A short, darkened upright mane runs down the neck. The ears are small and narrow and the mouth and muzzle are pointed. The eyes are on the side of the head and the pupils are elongated horizontally—this increases the eland's peripheral vision. A tuft of black hair is present on the male's forehead, which gets longer and thicker with age.

Black and white leg markings are present. The hooves are rounded and scent glands are found above the hooves on the hind legs—this allows the eland to leave a scent trail for any that have wandered away from the herd.

The tail is long with a tuft of long black hair on the tip.

Both sexes have long, black spiralled horns with a sharp point.

Elands have excellent hearing and a keen sense of smell.

Head & Body Length:	Male	2.4-3.4m
	Female	2-2.8m
Shoulder Height:	Male	1.5-1.8m
	Female	1.2-1.5m
Tail Length:		50 -90 cm
Length of Horns:		60-65cm
Weight:	Male	400-1000kg
	Female	300-600kg

Habitat

The eland is adaptable and is usually found in semi-deserts, savannahs, grasslands, miombo woodlands and mountainous regions up to 4,600m.

Behaviour

Elands are gregarious, non territorial, nomadic antelopes living in loosely formed herds of 30-80 individuals that roam over large areas, particularly during the dry season. Membership of the herd is fluid and constantly changes.

Females live together either in a small, all-female group or with a group of females and their offspring. Males live together in small all-male groups of three to four individuals in which there is a dominance hierarchy based on size, strength and age. Older males are usually solitary. Elands are shy and docile and if disturbed they quietly disappear, but when threatened will make a very hasty retreat.

Elands are sedentary and despite their cumbersome appearance they can run at speeds of 40km/h. They also have sufficient stamina to maintain a steady trot indefinitely and have the ability when required to jump 2-3m high in the air from a standing position.

Males are more sedentary than females.

Elands are diurnal and nocturnal.

Diet

Elands are adaptable herbivores and are browsers and grazers. They browse on leaves, branches, bark, berries, fruit and seed pods, and graze on grasses, tubers, bulbs and roots. If water is in short supply the eland is capable of extracting sufficient moisture from the plants it feeds on to meet its needs.

Communication

Elands use a variety of vocalisations, visual signals, bodily postures, movement and scent marking to communicate with each other.

Reproduction

The eland is polygamous and breeds throughout the year. The majority of the births take place before the start of the rainy season. During the mating season the males (bucks) become increasingly possessive towards sexually receptive females (does) and will fend off potential rivals. The gestation period is 280 days. The female gives birth to a single calf, which is hidden in vegetation for up to two weeks before being introduced into a nursery where it joins the other calves. The calves spend a lot of time establishing bonds by grooming and licking each other. Adult females present in the nursery group protect and defend the calves.

The calf is weaned by the time it is six months old. It will remain in the nursery group until it is two years old after which it will join a single sex group.

Females are sexually mature between 30-36 months old.

Males are sexually mature between 4-5 years old.

Predators/Threats

Elands are natural prey for African wild dogs, lions, leopards, cheetahs and hyenas. They are also hunted by humans for their hide and rich tasting meat.

Trivia

♦The eland is also known as the *southern eland*.

♦Elands are depicted in early East African rock art.

♦Attempts have been made to domesticate elands but this has proved extremely difficult as they like to roam over large areas. With persistence they do adapt and are able to mate in captivity. Their meat is considered to be rich and tasty and their milk is highly nutritious due to the high fat and protein content.

♦Elands are able to conserve water through raising their body temperature by as much as 7°C.

Coke's Hartebeest
(Alcelaphus buselaphus)
Swahili: *Kongoni*

Identification

The hartebeest is a large antelope, renowned for its speed and endurance when pursued.

The hartebeest appears awkward, cumbersome and ungainly. It has a sloping back with humped up shoulders that are higher than the hindquarters. The legs are long and slender.

The coat is long and fine and is a light tan/fawn colour. The hair on the chest, underside, legs and rump is much lighter in colour. Males are darker than females. The tail is relatively short with a tassel of long, black hair.

The hartebeest has a long head. The eyes are set high on the narrow face, with glands present beneath each one. The ears are long, narrow and pointed.

Both sexes have horns that arise from a pedicle on the forehead. The horns are short, ringed, curve upwards and backwards and have sharp tips.

The hartebeest has good eyesight and a keen sense of smell.

Body Length: 1.5-2.45m
Shoulder Height: 1.1-1.5m
Tail: 30-70cm
Weight: 120-220kg
Horns: 30-70cm

Life Span
Between 10-15 years in the wild.

Habitat
Hartebeest are usually found in savannahs, grasslands, open forests and woodlands up to an altitude of 2,000m.

Behaviour
Hartebeest are sociable, sedentary, peace-loving animals that live in mixed herds. These herds can on occasions contain up to 300 individuals and are comprised of:

74

Females and their offspring that have formed small to medium-sized herds of 5-20 individuals moving freely between territories. Females remain with their mother until they give birth to their own offspring.

Bachelor herds made up of young males who have left their mothers by the time they are 20 months old. They will attempt to take over and establish their own territory when they are three to four years old. Males defend their territory aggressively when challenged, and particularly during the breeding season. The boundary of the territory is marked with urine and dung heaps placed at regular intervals. Males lose their territory after seven to eight years and live in solitary isolation.

Non-territorial adult males.

Territorial males who may be solitary.

Because of their sedentary nature hartebeest are conspicuous and easy prey for predators and hunters. When feeding they have a lookout on duty who will warn of approaching danger by snorting loudly. When the need arises they are able to run at speeds of 70-80km/h, usually remaining in single file.

Hartebeest are diurnal. They are active early morning and late afternoon.

Diet
The hartebeest is a herbivore and a pure grazer that is able to feed on medium height grasses of poor quality. It is water-dependent and needs to drink daily.

Communication
A variety of vocalisations, visual signals, scent marking, tactile and territorial behaviours are used to communicate with each other.

Reproduction
Hartebeest are polygamous and breed all year round. The peak season for giving birth is in the dry season. During the mating season the male is preoccupied sniffing females' genitals, checking to see if they are in oestrus before proceeding to mate.

The gestation period is 214–242 days. The female gives birth to a single calf in a secluded spot. The calf is hidden in dense undergrowth for two weeks, with the female returning several times a day to feed it. Females remain with the maternal herd until they give birth.

Hartebeest reach sexual maturity between 18-30 months old.

Predators/Threats

They are natural prey for African wild dogs, lions, leopards, hyenas and jackals, and the young are preyed on by cheetahs. They are hunted by humans for their meat. Loss of habitat and competition for grass with domestic livestock are a threat to the hartebeest's survival.

Trivia

♦The hartebeest was used in sacrificial ceremonies by the ancient Egyptians.

♦The meat is apparently delicious and tastes like venison.

♦Hartebeests are rarely seen in zoos as they are difficult to breed and are a danger to each other and humans when in small confined places.

♦Despite the short length of its horns the hartebeest is capable of using them to kill.

Grant's Gazelle
(Gazella granti)
Swahili: *Swala granti*

Identification

The Grant's gazelle is a medium-sized antelope, often found grazing alongside the Thomson's gazelle.

The upper coat is a pale fawn colour, while the inside of the legs, the rump and the underside of the body are white. The white markings present on the rump extend to above the tail. A fine black stripe encircling the white rump is sometimes present on the female. The skin on the female's teats is coloured black, and white hair is present on the udder. The legs are long and slender.

The eyes are large, and the ears are long and pointed. A white stripe with a black outer edge extends from the horn to the muzzle. There is a white patch under the throat.

Both sexes have long, black-ringed horns that curve backwards and then forwards in an S shape.

Grant's gazelles have excellent eyesight and hearing.

Males are larger than females.

Body Length: 1.4-1.6m
Shoulder Height: 75-90cm
Weight: 38-82kg
Tail Length: 20-28cm
Horns: 45-80cm

Life Span

Between 10-14 years in the wild.

Habitat

Usually found in savannahs, grasslands and semi-desert areas up to an altitude of 2,500m, they avoid areas where there is tall grass. They are extremely tolerant of dry habitats.

Behaviour

Grant's gazelles are sociable animals living either in small herds of females with their young (10-25 individuals), all-male bachelor herds or territorial males. Membership of the herds is fluid and is constantly

changing. When food is plentiful the herds may merge and number several hundred, but as food becomes scarce the herds fragment.

Grant's gazelles are territorial. During the breeding season males mark their territories with secretions from glands located on their face, groin, knees and feet, as well as using urine and faeces. The territorial male defends its territory, and actively seeks to retain any females or groups of females that randomly stray into its territory. Young males are tolerated in the herd as long as they ignore the females.

The Grant's gazelle's agility and ability to run at speeds of 76-80km/h help them to outrun their predators. While on the run they leap high in the air with all four legs leaving the ground, and this alerts other gazelles to the presence of predators.

The Grant's gazelle is diurnal and nocturnal.

Diet

Being migratory herbivores they graze on succulent, short green grasses and shoots, and browse on herbs, shrubs, leaves, fruit and berries. They are water independent and are able to get all of the necessary moisture from the plants that they feed on.

Communication

They are quiet animals and use bodily postures to communicate with each other, this can include squatting while defecating and passing urine that warns off other males, leaping high into the air with all four legs leaving the ground to alert other gazelles of predators, and scent marking for territory identification using urine and dung heaps. Young males engage in fighting, but with age they use ritualised postures (feet stamping, bucking and rearing up).

Reproduction

Grant's gazelles are polygamous. Births peak in the months of January and August. The gestation period is 196 days and the female gives birth to a single fawn in tall grass. The female returns several times a day to feed the fawn. The fawn remains hidden in the grass for two to six weeks before joining the herd. They are weaned by the time they are six months old. Males leave the maternal herd when they are 12 months old to join bachelor herds, this also prevents in-breeding.

Females are sexually mature between 9-12 months old.

Males are sexually mature between 18-24 months old.

Predators/Threats

Grant's gazelles are natural prey for lions, cheetahs, leopards, African wild dogs, pythons and hyenas. The young are preyed upon by jackals. They are hunted by humans for their meat and hide. Loss of habitat is also a threat to their survival.

Trivia

♦Grant's gazelles are tolerant of high temperatures and drought conditions.

♦If the bodily temperature rises above that of the brain, a combination of panting and air-cooled blood circulating through the nose will reduce the overall temperature.

♦It is thought that the white underside helps to deflect the heat radiated from the ground.

Impala
(*Aepyceros melampus*)
Swahili: *Swala pala*

Identification
The impala is a slender, elegant medium-sized antelope.

The impala has a short, smooth, glossy top coat that is a pale, chestnut brown colour and has tan-coloured flanks. The underside and buttocks are white. A narrow, vertical black stripe is present on both rumps. The tail is small and white with a single black stripe down the centre.

The neck is long and slender. The ears are very large with black marking on the tips and white hair inside. White hair is present on the eyebrow, the chin and upper throat. The large eyes are encircled by white hair.

The impala has long, slender legs with hoofed feet. The hind legs have a tuft of coarse black hair posteriorly above the hooves, which covers a scent gland.

The male impala has lyre-shaped, ridged, ringed horns that continue to grow throughout life. The tips of the horns become shiny with age. Females do not have horns.

The impala has a keen sense of sight, smell and hearing.

The female impala is slightly smaller than the male.

Body Length:	1.2-1.6m
Shoulder Height:	75–99cm
Tail Length:	30-45cm
Weight:	40-80kg
Horns:	45-92cm

Life Span
Up to 15 years in the wild.

Habitat
Impalas are usually found in savannahs, grasslands, open forests and woodlands with little undergrowth. They are always found near water and avoid areas with tall grasses.

80

Behaviour

Impalas live in single-sexed herds. Males live in herds of up to 30 individuals. Females and offspring are found in herds of between 10-50 individuals, but herds can be as large as 200. If they wander into a male's territory, when they attempt to leave, the male will try to stop them but is rarely successful.

When food is plentiful, and during the rutting season, the dominant male becomes highly territorial and will round up any females that enter its territory. They mark their territory with urine, dung heaps (middens) and with a scent that is excreted from facial glands. The dominant male will defend its territory aggressively with bodily postures, threatening behaviour and loud vocalisations. Young males congregate in bachelor herds and are allowed to remain in the dominant male's territory as long as they ignore the females.

During dry periods the territories are abandoned and large herds of male and females form and go in search of food together.

Impala are prey to all major predators. They are extremely agile, and are able to leap 2.5m high in the air and jump distances of 9m. When frightened and alarmed the herd scatters in all directions, usually in the direction of dense vegetation. Their constant dodging, twisting, turning and change of direction, confuses the predators and enables them to outrun them. The impala can run at speeds of 64km/h.

Impala are primarily diurnal but are also considered to be nocturnal.

Diet

Impalas are adaptable herbivores, and are grazers and browsers. Grazing on young succulent grasses during the rainy season, and browsing on herbs, shrubs, seed pods, fruit, blossom and leaves during the dry season. During the dry season they need to drink daily.

Communication

Impalas are very vocal and use a variety of vocalisation to communicate with each other from grunting, roaring to snorting. Visual signals, scent marking and bodily postures (tail raising) are also used. When threatened, intimidated or required to assert their dominance they will utilise antagonistic, aggressive (chasing, fighting, herding) behaviours.

81

Reproduction

Impala are polygamous. Mating (rutting) takes place between March and June and lasts for three weeks. Dominant males (bucks) are highly territorial during the rutting season. They will try to separate and keep any females (does) that are in oestrus, that wander into their territory so that they can mate with them. The males are  able to detect females that are in oestrus by smelling and tasting their urine.

The male expends an enormous time and energy defending his territory from rival males, and rounding up and keeping the females together in the herd. The more females in the herd, the more time the male has to spend on keeping them together. The male is particularly vocal during this period. At the end of three months the male retires, exhausted, to recuperate in a bachelor group. After the mating season, other males are allowed to join the herd.

The gestation period is up to 200 days. The female gives birth to a single fawn in a secluded spot. The fawn is able to walk shortly after birth and is usually isolated from the herd for several days before been introduced into a nursery, where it joins the other fawns. The young fawns are vulnerable and are safer in a group, as it is more difficult for a predator to isolate and pick one out. Maternal bonds are weak and the only contact the fawn has with its mother is when it is suckled and when predators are about. The young are weaned between four to six months, after which, any existing maternal bonds completely disappear. Young males are forced to leave the maternal herd between six and eight months old and join a bachelor group. They are unable to  hold a territory until they are six years old. Females usually remain with the maternal herd.

Females reach sexual maturity at one year old. Males reach sexual maturity at 18 months old.

Predators/Threats

Impalas are common, and are natural prey for lions, leopards, cheetahs, caracal, hyenas, African wild dogs, jackals, crocodiles and pythons. The young are preyed on by baboons and martial eagles. They are hunted by humans for their meat and hide. Loss of habitat is a threat to their survival.

Trivia

♦The female impala can delay the birth of the fawn between two to four weeks until climatic and environmental conditions are more favourable.

♦Impala use designated areas to excrete in.

♦When it rains, impalas stop feeding and stand close together, with their backs to the wind.

♦Hunters use impala as bait when hunting leopards.

♦When the impala leaps into the air, scent is released from a special scent gland above the hoof which enables other impala in flight to pick up and follow its trail.

♦The meat of the impala is tender and sweet. It can be tenderised in pineapple juice for 30 minutes covered with papaya leaves.

Kirk's Dik-Dik
(*Madoqua kirkii*)
Swahili: *Digidigi funo/Dikidiki/Digidigi/Dika mbwa/Dik dik*

Identification
The dik-dik is a cloven-hoofed, miniature antelope.

The dik-dik's upper coat area is a yellowish grey to reddish brown colour. The underside, flanks and legs are lighter.

The head is large, in comparison to the size of its body. There is a small, upright tuft of hair on the top of its head that conceals two small, pointed, ringed horns. The horns slope backwards and are only present in the male. The ears are large.

White hair surrounds the large dark eyes, and is found beneath the chin. On the inner corner of each eye there is black spot under which lies a specialised preorbital gland that secretes a dark sticky substance. The dik-dik is able to scent mark its territory by inserting either a twig or grass stem into this gland.

The pointed, elongated snout is mobile and has nostrils that point downwards. A combination of blood flowing through the snout that is air cooled, and panting, helps to lower the dik-dik's bodily temperature and minimise water loss.

The dik-dik has delicate, spindle-like legs with small rubbery hooves that help to maintain its grip and balance when running over uneven, rocky ground.

The dik-dik has a short tail.

The dik-dik has excellent eyesight, hearing and sense of smell.

Female dik-diks are slightly larger than the males.

Head & Body Length:	55-72cm
Shoulder Height:	30-45cm
Tail Length:	4-9cm
Weight:	2.7-6.5kg
Horns:	4-11cm

Life Span
Three to four years in the wild.

Habitat

Dik-diks are found in a variety of locations ranging from savannahs, open plains to dense forests. They need low-growing, dense ground cover to feed on, and to hide in from predators. Always alert and on the lookout for predators, if the grasses and shrubs grow too tall for them to see over, they will move on.

Behaviour

Dik-diks are shy, graceful, elusive animals that spend a lot of time hiding in the bush. Dik-diks are territorial and both sexes scent mark the territory with secretions from glands on their feet and head, urine and faeces. Their dung heaps (middens) can be up to 30cm in diameter and are used regularly. Only the male defends the family territory. Well-used, worn trails through the bush form part of their territory.

The dik-dik is a vigilant, agile animal that reacts to the alarm call of other animals. It usually zig zags from side to side if startled and on the run. If in danger it can reach speeds of 42km/h but more often than not it will go into hiding. When the danger has passed by, dik-diks rub noses and begin scent-marking their territory.

Dik-diks are primarily nocturnal, but are considered to be diurnal as well. They feed early morning and late afternoon and rest at midday.

Diet

Dik-diks are adaptable herbivores, and are grazers and browsers, grazing on succulent grasses and browsing on roots, tubers, herbs, shrubs, shoots, leaves, buds, fruit and berries. The dik-dik is not water-dependent and is able to extract sufficient moisture from the plants it feeds on to meet its needs.

Communication

Dik-diks use a variety of vocalisations to communicate with each other. Visual signals, bodily postures, movement and scent marking are also used.

Reproduction

Dik-diks are monogamous and give birth to two litters a year, in the months of November-December and April-May. Although the female (ewe) does not seek to mate outside the life-long, bonded pair, the male (ram) will guard and protect her from other males when she is in oestrus.

The gestation period is up to 174 days. The female gives birth to a single fawn, which is suckled within 15 minutes of being born. The fawn is hidden in dense undergrowth for two to six weeks. The hiding place may change every few days. The female returns several times a day to feed the fawn. The male regularly licks and grooms the fawn. The young are weaned after three to four months and are fully grown by seven months old. Remaining with their mother until the next young is born, they are then forcibly driven away by either parent to find a mate and establish their own territory.

Females reach sexual maturity between six to eight months old. Males reach sexual maturity between eight to twelve months old.

Mortality for the young is 50%.

Predators/Threats

Dik-diks are natural prey for baboons, leopards, lions, cheetahs, hyenas, jackals, African wild dogs, crocodiles, monitor lizards, eagles and pythons. The young are preyed upon by baboons, eagles and genet cats. They are hunted by humans for their hide.

Trivia

♦The dik-dik is able to survive long periods without water, consequently their faeces are very dry and hard, and the urine is concentrated.

♦Salt is important to a dik-dik's diet and wellbeing.

♦The dik-dik makes a whistling noise when disturbed, which alerts the other animals to the presence of predators or hunters.

♦The small, slender bones of the legs and feet are used to make decorative jewellery.

♦The dik-dik gets its name from the noise it makes when alarmed.

Thomson's Gazelle
(Eudorcas thomsoni/Gazella thomsoni)
Swahili: *Swala tomi*

Identification

The Thomson's gazelle is a medium-sized antelope. It is the smallest gazelle, and the second fastest land animal after the cheetah.

The Thomson's gazelle's upper coat is a light tan-fawn colour. The chest and underside are white. A broad, black, horizontal stripe runs along the side of the body from the shoulders as far as the flank. The legs are long and slender with a long ankle and foot bones.

The white patch on the rump, which is bordered by an extremely fine black stripe, extends to just beneath the short black tail.

The head is small in comparison to the size of its body. The ears are large and the eyes, also large, are encircled by white hair. A broad, black band extends from below each eye, across the cheeks as far as the upper corner of the mouth. There is a distinct dark patch above the nose, which lightens as it extends upwards towards the forehead. The muzzle is narrow and the chin and under throat are an off-white colour.

The male has long, pointed, ringed horns that curve backwards, but with tips that gently curve forwards. Horns are usually absent on the female, but if they are present they are short and narrow.

Thomson's gazelles have excellent eyesight, hearing and a keen sense of smell.

Males are slightly bigger than females.

Length:	81cm-1.2m	
Shoulder Height:	56-68cm	
Tail Length:	15-20cm	
Weight:	Male	17-30kg
	Female	12-24kg
Horns:	Male	25-43cm
	Female	8-15cm

Life Span
Between 10 and 15 years in the wild.

Habitat

Thomson's gazelles like open spaces and are usually found in savannahs, grasslands, open plains and woodlands. They always live near water.

Behaviour

Thomson's gazelles are sociable animals living in all-female herds with their young, all-male herds, or mixed herds of up to 200 individuals. Membership of the herds is fluid and can change by the hour.

Travelling alongside wildebeest and zebras while searching for food and water, they are involved in the annual cyclical migration from the Serengeti to the Maasai Mara. Their numbers may be as high as 500,000.

Thomson's gazelles are territorial animals. Males, who usually remain territorial throughout their adult life, scent-mark their boundaries with urine and dung heaps (middens), and by depositing secretions on blades of grass from a small pre-orbital scent gland situated beneath each eye.

The male will regularly engage in combat fights to establish dominance and defend its territory, especially during the breeding season. Young males are tolerated in a herd as long as they ignore the females. The dominant male will attempt to retain any females who randomly stray into his territory.

Thomson's gazelles are prey to all of the major predators. They are extremely graceful and agile and are able to leap 3m high and jump distances of 9m. The Thomson's gazelle's ability to run at speeds of 65-80km/h and outrun the predators, as well as constantly dodging, twisting, turning and changing direction quickly, makes them extremely difficult prey to catch. While on the run they leap high in the air with all four legs leaving the ground; this alerts other gazelles to the presence of predators.

The Thomson's gazelle is diurnal and nocturnal. They are active early morning and late afternoon.

Diet

Thomson's gazelles are migratory herbivores and are primarily a grazer feeding on succulent, short green grasses, but when these are absent they will browse on shoots, shrubs, seeds and leaves. They are water-dependent and need to drink every one to two days, particularly in the dry season, however if the need arises they are able to extract sufficient moisture from the plants they feed on.

Communication

Thomson's gazelles are unusually quiet and use bodily postures (holding their head high, pointing in the direction of predators), visual displays (contracting the underlying skin of the horizontal black body band to increase its size and make it more visible), stamping feet, scent marking and the occasional snort to communicate with each other.

Reproduction

Thomson's gazelles are polygamous and may give birth to two litters each year. The peak season for giving birth is after the rainy season.

The gestation period is between 150-185 days. The female leaves the herd to find a secluded spot to give birth to a single fawn. Occasionally two fawns are born. The fawn is hidden in long grass for up to three weeks, it is particularly vulnerable at this point in time to predation and must remain perfectly still to avoid being detected. The female returns several times a day to feed the fawn. As soon as it is able to run, it will join the herd. The fawn is weaned by the time it is four months old. To prevent in-breeding, males leave the maternal herd to join a bachelor herd.

Mortality for the young is as high as 50%.

Predators/Threats

Thomson's gazelles are natural prey for lions, cheetahs, leopards, African wild dogs, jackals and crocodiles. The young are preyed upon by baboons, birds of prey, jackals, pythons and serval cats. They are hunted by humans for their meat and hide.

Trivia

♦The Thomson's gazelle is nicknamed "Tommie".

♦The Thomson's gazelle is similar in appearance to the Grant's gazelle, but is easily distinguished by the horizontal black band on its side.

♦The Thomson's gazelle is named after the Scotsman Joseph Thomson who explored Africa in the 1890s.

♦The Thomson's gazelle's tail is in continuous motion, swinging to and fro and from side to side.

Topi
(Damaliscus lunatus)
Swahili: *Nyemera/Paa*

Identification
The topi is a hardy, medium-sized antelope that has a distinctive appearance and colouration.

The topi looks awkward and ungainly with its short neck, humped shoulders, sloping back and long slender legs. The black head is long and narrow, with a narrow muzzle that has tan-coloured lips. The ears are narrow and slender.

The topi's glossy coat is a red-purple-brown colour with blue-purple patches straddling the flanks, shoulders and upper legs. The lower half of the legs are a gingery tan colour. The rump and tail are paler. A tuft of hair is present on the tail.

Both sexes have thick, ringed, lyre-shaped horns.

Female topis are a lighter colour.

The topi has good eyesight and hearing.

Body Length:	1.5-2.0m
Shoulder Height:	1-1.3m
Tail Length:	40-60cm
Weight:	75-160kg
Horns:	72cm

Habitat
Topis are usually found in lowlands, savannahs, flood plains, woodlands and semi deserts.

Behaviour
The topi is sociable and territorial and often found in close proximity to other herds of antelopes.

Females live in small herds of between 15-20 individuals, with their offspring and a single, dominant male. Males either live in loosely formed bachelor herds of between 8-20 individuals, or they can be solitary. The herds merge temporarily when migrating to form mega herds. Whenever the herds stop moving, the males begin to establish small territories and round up the females.

91

Males become territorial between the ages of four to five years old and mark their territory with urine, dung heaps (middens) and secretions from their pre-orbital glands. They spend a considerable amount of time on their own, overseeing and guarding their territory, usually on the summit of a termite mound.

Topis are able to run at speeds of up to 70km/h if required.

The topi is diurnal.

Diet

Topis are highly selective herbivores that graze on grass and very rarely on leaves. They have a preference for succulent green grass. If they eat dry, coarse grasses they need long rest periods to chew their cud in order to aid digestion. Topis are able to survive for long periods without water providing they have access to succulent green grass, otherwise they will need to drink daily.

Communication

Topis use a variety of vocalisations, visual signals, bodily postures, movement and scent marking to communicate with each other.

Reproduction

Mating is dependent on favourable weather conditions and availability of food. During the breeding season the male establishes small territories and rounds up as many females as possible to mate with. The dominant male is easily recognised as he struts around with an upright posture and head held high.

The gestation is between 225-240 days. If environmental and climatic conditions are not favourable the female is able to delay the birth of the calf. The female gives birth to a single calf, which is hidden in vegetation for between 3-12 days before joining a kindergarten; the females take it in turn to watch over the calves while the others go in search of food. The calf, which has a sandy brown coat, is able to walk within 15 minutes of being born. Horns appear when they are three months old, and at the same time their coat begins to take on the adult

colouration. Weaning is complete by the time the calf is four months old.

Females reach sexual maturity between 18-24 months old.

Males reach sexual maturity between 36-48 months old.

Predators/Threats

Topis are natural prey for cheetahs, lions, leopards and African wild dogs. The topi is a highly selective herbivore that feeds almost entirely on grass—this means that when there is a lack of available grass, or competition for grass from other herbivores, the topi will be at risk of starvation. Loss of habitat is a threat to the topi's survival. Topis are hunted by humans, despite being difficult to catch.

Trivia

♦The topi is also known as the *sassaby*.

♦If the topi is lucky and does not fall foul of predators, it will die when its teeth fall out.

♦Male topis usually live a solitary life, and even if part of a herd they will be on their own overseeing, patrolling and guarding the territory - this makes them more likely to be taken by predators.

Waterbuck

Common or Ringed Waterbuck *(Kobus ellipsiprymnus ellipsiprymnus)*
Defassa Waterbuck *(Kobus ellipsiprymnus defassa)*
Swahili: *Kuro*

Identification

The waterbuck is a large, robust, muscular antelope.

The coat is long, coarse and shaggy. Sweat glands in the skin secrete an oily, brown, tar-like substance that waterproofs the coat. It has a distinct, lingering odour—described as musk-like.

There are two species of waterbucks in Kenya and Tanzania:

The <u>common waterbuck</u>, which is greyish brown in colour. It has a distinct, circular white ring on its rump that encircles the tail, with a darker patch in the centre.

The <u>defassa waterbuck</u>, which is reddish brown in colour. It has a solid, white circular patch on either side of its rump.

Males are darker than females. The colour of the body darkens with age.

The short, strong legs are darker in colour than the body, and there are white rings above the hooves

The waterbuck has a long body with a straight back. The ears are large, prominent and rounded. The eyes are placed on either side of the head, and horizontal, elongated pupils allow for all-round, peripheral vision. White hair is present above the eyes, inside the ears and on the muzzle. There is a rough mane around the neck, and a creamy-white patch under the throat.

The male waterbuck has long, pointed, spiral, ringed horns that sweep up and back. The female does not have horns.

Waterbucks have excellent eyesight and a keen sense of smell and hearing.

Head & Body length:	1.7-2.3m
Shoulder Height:	1m-1.4m
Weight:	Male 200-300kg
	Female 150-200kg
Tail Length:	22-45cm
Horns:	55-100cm

Life Span
Between 14-18 years in the wild.

Habitat
Waterbuck are usually found in savannahs, grasslands, forests and woodlands. They are always found near water.

Behaviour
Waterbucks are quiet, sedentary, territorial animals. They are not migratory, and usually remain within the same home range year round, living in herds of between 5-30 individuals. Membership of the herd is fluid and changes day to day.

Young males (bulls) form bachelor herds of between five to ten individuals from the age of two years old. This is a hierarchical closely knit group based on seniority, size and strength. Remaining in the herd until they have matured, which is between the ages of six to seven years old, they then become territorial.

The females (cows) and calves live in a loosely formed nursery group of between 5-25 individuals. A dominant male may or may not be present. Females may also be seen alone or in pairs. Mature, dominant males are territorial, and will try to keep any females that stray into their domain, although they are rarely successful.

The dominant male aggressively defends his territory until the age of ten. The territory is not scent marked, as their bodily odour is sufficient to advertise their presence.

Waterbucks are nocturnal and diurnal. They feed early morning and late afternoon.

Diet
The waterbuck is a herbivore, it is primarily a grazer but will also browse, grazing on a variety of medium and short coarse grasses, and browsing on herbs and leaves from shrubs and trees. Waterbucks are water-dependent and need to drink daily.

Communication
Waterbucks use a variety of vocalisations, visual signals, bodily postures and movement to communicate with each other.

Reproduction

Waterbucks are polygamous and breed all year round. The peak season for giving birth is in the rainy season. The dominant male may have a harem of cows and may be challenged by other males for mating rights.

The gestation period is up to 280 days. Several days before the birth, the female finds a secluded spot away from the herd, and gives birth to a single calf. Within 30 minutes of being born the calf is able to stand up and walk. The calf is hidden in dense thickets and long grass for two to four weeks, with the female returning several times a day to feed it. Each time she leaves the calf, she grooms it thoroughly to remove any lingering odours that may attract predators. The young are weaned after six to seven months. Horns first appear on the male when they are eight to nine months old. The young males wander off to join all male groups but the females remain with the maternal group.

Females reach sexual maturity between 12-14 months old. Males reach sexual maturity between 14-18 months old.

Predators/Threats

Waterbucks are natural prey for lions, leopards, cheetahs, hyenas, jackals, wild dogs and crocodiles. Loss of habitat is a threat to their survival. They have been known to be hunted for their meat.

Trivia

♦The meat of the waterbuck is tough, and has an unpleasant odour and taste; it is believed that this deters many potential predators.

♦The waterbuck is the most water-dependent of all the antelopes.

♦Waterbucks are strong swimmers and take refuge in water if threatened by predators.

♦The waterbuck's long shaggy hair attract ticks and they are prone to foot-and-mouth disease, anthrax and rinderpest.

Wildebeest
(*Connochaetes taurinus*)
Swahili: *Nyumbu Ya Montu*

Identification

The wildebeest is a large antelope and is synonymous with the annual migration of animals from the Serengeti in Tanzania to the Maasai Mara in Kenya and back.

The wildebeest has a long, black, narrow head with large nostrils, and a wide muzzle equipped with incisors suited to eating short grass quickly. It has a shaggy mane of long, black, thick hair and a beard that goes underneath the throat. The ears are long and narrow.

The coat is short and glossy and is a grey-brown colour. Males are darker in colour than females. Vertical bands of long black hair are present on the neck and forequarters.

The cow-like horns are long, curved and sharp. The horns of the male are larger than the female's and are joined by a shield (*boss*) that covers the forehead.

The wildebeest looks cumbersome and ungainly with muscular, heavily built forequarters and disproportionately slender hindquarters. The legs are long and spindle-like with hooves. They are agile and able to run at 65km/h.

The tail is long, black and hairy.

Wildebeest have good eyesight, sense of hearing and smell.

Length:		2.4-3.4m
Shoulder Height:	Male	1.25-1.45m
	Female	1.15-1.42m
Tail:		45-56cm
Weight:	Male	165-300kg
	Female	140-230kg
Horns	Male	55-80cm
	Female	45-63cm

Life Span
Twenty years in the wild.

Habitat

Wildebeest are usually found in grasslands, plains and open woodland. They are always found near water.

Behaviour

Wildebeest are sociable and territorial, living in herds that are constantly on the move searching for fresh food and water. The wildebeest that live in the Serengeti are migratory and are renowned for their annual, cyclical migration from the Serengeti to the Maasai Mara. Trekking over 19km a day alongside the zebras and antelopes, 250,000 wildebeest will perish — the very young, lame, sick and old.

Wildebeest live in mixed herds (within a mega herd) comprised of:

Bachelor herds made up of young males and bulls without territories that live on the fringes of the herd. Males (bulls) leave the bachelor herd when they are four to five years old and become territorial.

Small herds of females (cows), calves and yearlings of 10-100 individuals. Males leave between the ages of one and two years old to join a bachelor herd.

Territorial bulls, who may be solitary.

As food becomes scarce the herds lose their individual identities and merge.

Territorial males mark the boundaries of their territory with dung heaps and secretions from their preorbital gland and hooves. When competing for territories either on their own or in small groups, territorial males display aggressive behaviours, grunting and bellowing, pawing the earth, standing erect and thrusting and tossing their horns about.

Wildebeest are primarily diurnal but can be considered nocturnal as well. They are active early morning and late afternoon.

Diet

The wildebeest is a nomadic herbivore, feeding on short grass. Wildebeest are water-dependent and need to drink every day.

Communication

Wildebeest are noisy animals and will use a variety of vocalisations to communicate with each other. Visual signals, scent marking, tactile behaviours (sniffing and touching noses, neck and genitals) are also used. When threatened or when they are required to assert their dominance, males will utilise agonistic (tilting their heads, horn sweeping, leaping, bucking and spinning) behaviours.

Reproduction

Wildebeest are polygamous. Mating begins at the end of the rainy season (March-April) with males competing for territories and females. The females will mate with several males during this period.

The gestation period is between 240-250 days with 80-90% of calves been born in a 2-3 week period in February and March. Although the young are easy prey for the predators, their high numbers (500,000 in the Serengeti) ensure that more of them will survive.

The female gives birth to a single calf, usually within the herd rather than in isolation, and almost always before midday. Within minutes of being born the calf is able to stand up and walk about and is able to keep up with the herd within two days. They are able to eat grass after ten days and are suckled between six to twelve months.

The female spends one to two days imprinting herself on the calf so that she is able to recognise its scent. The calves are initially a light brown colour but by the time they are nine weeks old they begin to take on the adult colouration. Their tiny horns are initially upright, but begin to grow sideways after they are eight months old. Calves remain close to their mothers, if they lose contact, they are actively rejected by all of the other females and their days are numbered. Males are driven away from the herd when the next calf is born, but females remain with the maternal herd.

Females are sexually mature between two and a half and three years old. Males are sexually mature between three and four years old.

Predators/Threats

Wildebeest are natural prey for lions, hyenas, cheetahs, leopards, African wild dogs and crocodiles. Loss of habitat is a threat to their survival.

Trivia

♦Wildebeest are sometimes referred to as *gnus*.

♦The majority of newborn wildebeest are female.

♦Wildebeest are the commonest animal to live on the African plains.

♦Wildebeest live in the highest concentration of all known mammals.

♦On an evening, wildebeest sleep in rows on the ground for safety and security.

♦Wildebeest live in enormous "mega" herds of up to 1 million animals.

Migration

The annual wildebeest migration across the plains of the Serengeti in Tanzania to the Masai Mara in Kenya and back is the greatest wildlife spectacle on earth. This is a never-ending, epic journey with the animals driven on in the relentless search for fresh food and water. It is a fight for survival. Trekking over 19km a day, 250,000 wildebeest will perish on this annual pilgrimage—the very young, lame, sick and old. Hot in the pursuit of the migration are the predators—carnivores and scavengers alike.

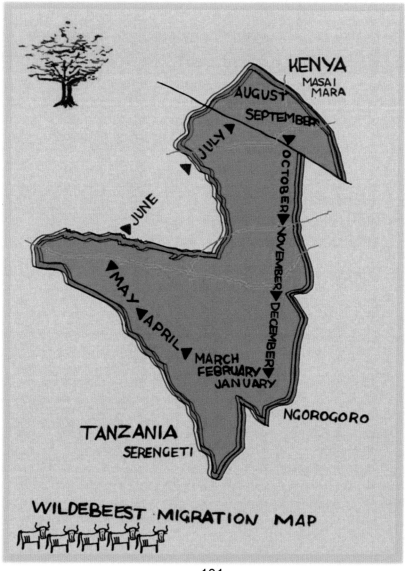

WILDEBEEST MIGRATION MAP

January-February

The months of January and February find over 1.5 million wildebeest and 300,000 zebras and antelopes congregated on the Salei and Ndutu plains, which are located in the southern part of the Serengeti, adjacent to the Ngorongoro Conservation Area.

Zebras give birth to their young in January. The wildebeest give birth to 500,000 calves within the space of two to three weeks in February.

March

March sees the arrival of the long rains from the north. The southern plains are stripped bare of grass and the migration needs to move on in search of food and water.

April-May

The migration travels northwards towards the central area of the Serengeti, with a large number of animals present in the Seronera, an area popular with safari operators. They continue through the long grass plains and woodlands towards the Western Corridor, alongside the Mbalageti River and towards the Grumeti Controlled Area, where the long rains have now set in.

Towards the end of May the rains die away and the rutting season begins.

June

The migration is now firmly established in the Western Corridor and crosses the Grumeti River towards the Ikorongo Controlled Area. Some animals travel in a different direction towards the Lobo area.

It is now the dry season.

July

The migration arrives at the Ikorongo Controlled area and proceeds to cross the notorious Mara River towards the Maasai Mara (Kenya). Many hundreds will die as they cross the river, searching for a safe and suitable crossing point, either breaking their legs on the sides of the steep, slippery banks or being trampled to death in the ensuing, panic-stricken stampede. Waiting eagerly, either in the water or the banks of the Mara River, are the Nile crocodiles who make quick work of any fallen prey.

The crossing of the Mara River is spectacular because of the high volume of water that is present, whereas the Grumeti River is made up of a series of intermittent pools and channels. The migratory herd now enters the Maasai Mara, in their continued search for food and water.

August-September

The migratory herds reside in the Maasai Mara from July through to October where there is a plentiful supply of water.

October-November

The migration slowly starts to leave the Maasai Mara, crossing the Mara River once again and heading towards the southern plains where the new rains are starting.

December

The migration continues moving back along the Loliondo boundary, towards the regenerated grasses of the southern plains They will remain in the southern plains throughout the months of January, February and March before the annual, cyclical migration begins once more.

Primates

Black-and-White Colobus Monkey
(Colobus guereza)
Swahili: *Mbega mweupe*

Identification
The fur of the colobus monkey is very distinct: glossy black with a long white mantle on the sides of the body, and a white beard that surrounds the face.

The skin on the face is hairless and grey in colour.

The tail is long and has a bushy white tuft at the tip.

Calluses on the rump allow the colobus monkey to sit for extended periods on tree branches.

Unlike other primates, the colobus monkey does not have a thumb, only four fingers which provide a strong grip allowing it to move quickly and gracefully from tree to tree.

Colobus monkeys are able to make amazing and spectacular leaps of up to 15m. through the tree tops. Their trailing black and white hair and long tail act as a parachute.

Head & Body Length:	45-72cm
Tail Length:	52cm-1m
Weight:	5-14kg

Life Span
Twenty years in the wild.

Habitat
Colobus monkeys are usually found in forests, woodlands or wooded grasslands, both in lowlands and coastal mountains (up to 3,300m), and along water courses in arid, savannah regions.

Behaviour
Colobus monkeys live in limited, well-defined territories. They are arboreal, and are rarely seen on the ground, spending the majority of

their time high up in the tree tops where they are extremely well camouflaged.

The troops are small and social, consisting of up to 15 animals made up of the dominant male, several females and their offspring. The females remain in the group for life. Young males leave the group before they reach sexual maturity, their departure may be voluntary or may be initiated by the lead male. These young males may lead solitary lives or band together with other males. Where territories overlap with other troops of colobus monkeys, they are vigorously defended by the males and this may involve physical contact. At nighttime they take it in turns to guard the troop and their territory from predators.

Colobus monkeys are diurnal.

Diet

Colobus monkeys are herbivores, and exist on a diet that consists mainly of leaves, blossom, leaf buds, flowers, fruit, stems, bark, twigs and aquatic plants.

Their large, complex, two-chambered stomachs support bacterial micro floral colonies and this allows them to digest large quantities of difficult, mature, toxic foliage. The leaves, although plentiful, are a source of low energy and nutrition and result in the colobus monkey being relatively inactive. Their dependence on foliage restricts them to forest habitations, however they will eat agricultural crops in inhospitable environments.

Communication

Male colobus monkeys are very noisy and vocal, particularly at dawn, and this is used as a means of communication to segregate the groups. Their calls are very distinctive, and have been described as: roars, snorts, purrs, honks and screams.

Visual signals and body postures are also used as a means of communication. Tactile communication includes social grooming, playing and fighting.

Reproduction

There is no distinct breeding season. Colobus monkeys are polygamous, and females initiate the mating process by attracting the male through lip smacking. The gestation period is six months and the female gives birth to only one offspring, which is born with its eyes open. For the first month the young have a pink face and their body is covered with white fur which soon begins to change colour, with the final black and white colour of adulthood being achieved by the age of six months.

The female suckles the young for one year, although the infant clings to both the mother's and father's abdomen. Both parents participate in rearing the young infant and may also involve other female members in the group. These substitute mothers, known as "allo" mothers, will suckle the young infant and also carry it around on their abdomen.

Females reach sexual maturity at between four to six years old. Males reach sexual maturity between four to eight years old.

Predators/Threats

Colobus monkeys are natural prey for hawk eagles, leopards and the occasional chimpanzee. They are hunted illegally for their beautiful fur and for their meat. Their skin is used to make dance costumes, hats and capes. The main threat to the colobus monkey's survival is loss of habitat as forests are cut down for logging, human habitation and agricultural purposes.

Trivia

♦*Colobus* is a Greek word that means "mutilated" or "docked", and refers to the absence of a thumb.

♦Colobus monkeys are sacred icons to the gods of the Hindu and Buddhist religions.

♦The colobus monkey is also affectionately known as the "Messenger of God", as it basks in the tree tops in the early morning and late afternoon sun.

Olive Baboon
(Papiocynocephalus anubis)
Swahili: *Nyani*

Identification
The olive baboon is the most widespread of the baboon family and gets its name from its dark green-grey colour.

The baboon has a large muscular body covered in thick, grey-green-brown fur. The female is duller than the male. The back slopes downwards and the males have a long tapering mane of hair around the neck. Calluses, which are thickened patches of skin, are present on the hairless rump. The tail is non-prehensile.

The baboon has a dog-like face with close-set eyes, a prominent eyebrow ridge and rounded ears. The hair on the face is fine and is dark grey to black in colour. The muzzle is hairless, long and pointed. The jaws are strong and powerful with long, pointed canine teeth up to 5cm long. Large cheek pouches enable the baboon to eat while on the move, as well as getting their fill when competing for scarce food.

The baboon has long, powerful arms and legs and is able to move about on four limbs. Five fingers are present on the hands of the arms, and five toes are present on the hind legs, all of which are used for grasping.

Males are larger than females.

Head and Body Length: 60-86cm
Tail: 41-58cm
Weight: 22-37kg

Life Span
Up to 30 years in the wild.

Habitat
Baboons are adaptable and are usually found in savannahs, grasslands, rocky areas, open woodlands, forests and semi-arid areas–all of which will be close to water.

Behaviour

Baboons are sociable and live in a highly organised, complex, hierarchical group of between 30-80 individuals, called a troop. These troops can be as large as 200 in number. The troop is made up of adult females and their offspring and adult males. There are several dominant males within the troop and each member has a ranked position.

The dominant male (alpha male) uses his physical prowess to protect, defend, dominate and maintain order within the troop, ultimately deciding on the movement of the troop, what they will eat and where they will sleep. A linear, hierarchical social order exists amongst the females, and is in order of birth and kin. This ensures that the dominant females' offspring assume the same privileges of social ranking.

Baboons are terrestrial, spending the majority of their time foraging for food early morning and late afternoon and resting at midday. When they are not foraging for food they sit in small groups grooming each other, looking for and removing parasites, dead skin and dirt. Grooming reinforces social bonds, with subordinates grooming dominant members. Males groom females in particular when they are seeking sexual access.

When threatened baboons may run away, but they are also capable of being quite ferocious—they will either bark or bare their large canine teeth, and have even been known to attack humans. Mobbing predators if the young are threatened, male baboons are a formidable force to be reckoned with and more than capable of inflicting serious injuries.

Baboons are diurnal and retreat to the safety of the trees, cliffs and rocky outcrops at night.

Diet

Baboons are omnivores. They are opportunistic foragers and feed primarily on aquatic plants, grasses, lichens, roots, tubers, bulbs, bark, bark sap, leaves, blossom, berries and seeds. They supplement their diet with insects, small mammals (rodents, vervet monkeys), birds, fish, shell fish, lizards and snakes. They need to drink water every day or two.

Communication

Being extremely noisy they use up to 30 vocalisations to communicate with each other, such as clicking, barking, grunting, roaring, screeching and screaming. Facial expressions or visual displays are used to communicate their mood and intention, these may be staring, smiling, baring teeth, raising eyebrows, narrowing eyes, yawning, head shaking and lip smacking. Bodily postures and tactile/sociable greetings (grooming, embracing each other, nose to nose greetings), are also used as a form of communication.

Reproduction

Baboons are promiscuous, breeding throughout the year with a multitude of partners. The female comes into heat once a month during which time the rump changes colour from grey to a bright pink. There is a lot of competition and aggression between the males to gain attention and access to the female at this time. The female initiates the mating process by presenting her pink swollen rump to the males. She gives birth to a single infant once a year, after a gestation period of 180 days. The infant is born with pink skin which darkens with age and is  covered in black fur. By the time the infant is six months old it will have taken on adult colouration and will be an olive green colour. The infant remains in close contact with its mother by clinging to her stomach for the first four weeks of its life, after which it will ride jockey style on her back, as well as that of other members of the troop. This continues until the infant is one year old. Both male and female care for the young, but the majority of the care is provided by the mother and other female members of the troop. Males will assist by gathering food and grooming.

By the time the infant is four to six months old it will be spending most of its time playing with the other juveniles. The young are weaned by the time they are one year old, and are independent by the time they are 18 months old.

Females are sexually mature between the ages of four to six years old and remain with the maternal group for life.

Males are sexually mature between the ages of five to seven years old. Before they reach sexual maturity they leave the maternal group to join a new troop, gaining acceptance into the new troop by befriending a female over many months.

Predators/Threats

Baboons are natural prey for African wild dogs, cheetahs, chimpanzees, crocodiles, hyenas, lions and leopards. They are hunted by humans if they are considered to be a pest by raiding crops and being present in large numbers. Loss of habitat is a threat to their survival.

Trivia

♦The olive baboon is also known as the *savannah baboon* or *Anubis baboob.*

♦Baboons have the same dental pattern and number of teeth as a human.

♦Baboons will wade into swamps for water lily tubers.

♦Baboons are fond of raiding agricultural crops.

Vervet Monkey
(*Cercopithecus aethiops*)
Swahili: *Tumbili/Ngedere*

Identification

The vervet or green monkey is a medium-sized primate.

The body is long and slender. The coarse dorsal fur is either a greyish olive-green or brown colour. The underside and the inside of the arms and legs are covered with white fur. The skin on the abdomen is blue.

Vervet monkeys have a small, hairless black face encircled by elongated whiskery white hair. The canines are long and sharp and there are cheek pouches for storing food.

The arms and legs are approximately the same length and this allows the vervet monkey to walk on all four limbs. The hands and feet are black and hairless.

The tail is long with a black tip that curves downwards when the tail is held upright.

The male has a bright blue scrotum and red penis.

Male vervet monkeys are larger than the females.

Height:	Males	45-85cm
	Females	40-60cm
Tail:		50 cm-1.1m
Weight:	Males	3.5-7.5kg
	Females	2.5-5.5kg

Habitat

Vervet monkeys are adaptable and widely distributed, and are found in savannahs, grasslands and woodlands up to altitudes of 3,000m, usually in close proximity to streams, rivers and lakes. They rarely stray more than 460m away from the safety of wooded areas.

Behaviour

Vervet monkeys are highly sociable and live together in a close-knit group called a troop of between 6-80 individuals, although the average troop size is 25. The troop is made up of one or more males, females and their offspring and has a highly developed hierarchical social order that dominates all aspects of the monkeys' lives. The dominant male (alpha) and female (matriarch) maintain their authority by using aggressive behaviours, and they are given priority when foraging for food, eating and when engaged in grooming.

The alpha male protects the troop and has access to all high ranking females. The alpha male has a second in command, the beta male, whose duty is to scout for food and warn the troop of the presence of intruders or predators. Other adult males are allowed to remain in the troop as long as they do not engage with the females.

The linear hierarchical social order that exists among the females is in order of birth and kin and ensures that the dominant females' offspring assume the same privileges of social ranking. Other adults are submissive to the juveniles that belong to a family of a higher social status. Physical affection is especially important among family members. Grooming in particular reinforces social bonds, with the monkeys spending many hours every day grooming each other, and looking for and removing parasites, dirt and dead skin.

Vervet monkeys are semi-arboreal and semi-terrestrial, spending the majority of their time during the day foraging for food on the ground.

They usually walk about on all fours but will stand upright on their hind legs to get a better view. On an evening they retreat to the safety of the trees to sleep.

When food is scarce both sexes become territorial and scent-mark their territory with secretions from their facial glands, by rubbing their chins and cheeks on trees and rocks. When there is an abundance of food they relax and concentrate on foraging.

Vervet monkeys are diurnal.

Diet

Vervet monkeys are omnivores and feed primarily on grasses, herbs, bulbs, roots, shoots, bark, leaves, buds, flowers, and fruit, supplementing their diet with small birds, eggs, insects and rodents. Close to human habitation they become a nuisance as they regularly raid vegetable plots, lodges and camp sites. Vervet monkeys need to drink water daily.

Communication

Vervet monkeys are very vocal and use a wide range of vocalisations to communicate with each other and their offspring, from barking, woofing, squealing, purring and chirping to grunting (19 sounds in total). Facial expressions (staring, head bobbing, rapid glancing), tactile communication (nose to nose touching), bodily postures (penile display) and tail signals are also used as an indication of their mood or the presence of predators.

Reproduction
Vervet monkeys breed throughout the year. Only the alpha male is allowed to mate with the females and he defends this right fiercely.

The gestation period is between 160-165 days. The majority of births take place at night, and during the rainy season when there is an abundance of food. The female gives birth to a single infant and is very protective towards her offspring. After licking the infant clean the female will bite off the umbilical cord and proceed to eat the afterbirth. The infant is born with its eyes open, a pink face and covered in black fur. The infant remains in close contact with its mother by clinging to her stomach for the first three weeks of its life, after which it will venture out to play with other youngsters. Fifty per cent of the infants do not make it to adulthood, they die from poor nutrition or predation.

Males do not participate in rearing the young, this is left to the mother, other siblings and females.

The young are weaned by the time they are six months old and are independent by the time they are one year old.

Females are sexually mature when they are four years old and begin to reproduce when they are five years old. Females remain with the maternal group.

Males are sexually mature when they are five years old, at which point they leave the maternal troop to go in search of another troop with no female relations. This is a difficult time as male outsiders are never welcome and meet with considerable aggression. Male vervet monkeys may change troops several times throughout their lives, always during the mating season.

Predators/Threats

Vervet monkeys are natural prey for lions, leopards, cheetahs, caracals, serval cats, baboons, eagles, crocodiles and pythons. They are hunted for their meat and are used in traditional medicine. They may be poisoned, trapped or shot when close to human habitation as they are seen as a pest regularly stealing food and raiding crops. Game farms may use vervet monkeys as target practice. Loss of habitat is a threat to their survival.

Trivia

◆Vervet monkeys are used in scientific research. Their tissue is used in the production of the smallpox and polio vaccine. They are especially useful in research into high blood pressure, cancer, organ transplants, immunology, pharmacology and psychology.

◆A bereaved mother will often keep the body of her infant with her for several days after its death.

◆Pythons usually wait at the bottom of a tree to ambush a vervet monkey as it climbs head first down a tree.

◆Vervet monkeys are able to swim.

◆Vervet monkeys are intelligent and possess cognitive skills, being able to demonstrate and express emotion through mime.

◆Vervet monkeys are particularly vulnerable to parasitic skin diseases.

Common Birds

Flamingo
Greater Flamingo (*Phoenicopterus roseus*)
Lesser Flamingo (*Phoenicopterus minor*)
Swahili: *Heroe*

Identification

There are six species of flamingo in the world, two of which are found in the African continent. They are the greater flamingo and the lesser flamingo.

The flamingo is a wading bird with long, pink, spindle-like legs and small webbed feet.

The large body is covered in pink feathers. The colour originates from the bacteria spirulina, which is found in the blue green algae of the salt water lakes, diatoms, small crustaceans and alpha and beta carotene.

The neck is long and flexible with a small head. The eyes are small and are a yellow-orange colour. The bare skin between the eyes and the beak is pink. The large, hook-shaped beak is pink with a black tip.

The flamingo has large wings and a short tail. A gland near the base of the tail produces an oil-like substance that the flamingo spreads over its feathers when preening.

Males are larger than females.

There are two species of flamingo present in Kenya and Tanzania:

Lesser Flamingo

The lesser flamingo is the commonest, smallest and brightest of all the flamingos. The lesser flamingo plumage is an evenly coloured deep pink. The bill is dark red with a black tip. The legs are red and a hind toe called a hallux is present.

Height:	90cm-1m
Wing Span:	99cm
Weight:	1.5-2kg

Greater Flamingo

The greater flamingo is the largest and most widespread of all the flamingos. The greater flamingo is taller than the lesser flamingo and is a pale whitish-pink colour with red patches. The primary and secondary feathers are black. The bill is pale pink with a black tip. The legs are pink.

Height:	1-1.5m
Wing Span:	1.3-1.6m
Weight:	2-4kg

Habitat
Flamingos live in areas of shallow salt water such as lakes, dams, lagoons, swamps, mangroves, estuaries, salt pans and tidal flats. They are able to live at high altitude and tolerate extreme ranges in temperature.

The lesser flamingo is found in Africa and India.

The greater flamingo is found Europe, Asia, Africa, North and South America.

Behaviour
Flamingos are nomadic birds that live in large, closely packed flocks all year round comprising tens of thousands of individuals.

Flamingos usually fly at night to avoid predators. Reaching speeds of 50-60km/h they are capable of covering long distances of up to 600km. Flying with their head, neck and legs outstretched they either fly in a V formation or in a single line. To become airborne the flamingo has to run forwards while flapping its wings, and when landing it will run several steps before it stops. When resting they always face into the wind to prevent the rain and wind penetrating their feathers, they rest by either sitting down with their legs tucked underneath them or by standing on one leg. It is not unusual to see a flock of flamingos floating on the surface of the water.

Diet
Flamingos are filter feeders that flourish in salt lakes. Webbed feet, which prevent the flamingo from sinking, disturb the underlying mud when searching for food. The beak of the flamingo turns sharply downwards two thirds along its length, this means that when feeding the head has to be lowered into the water in an upside down position allowing it to ladle up water and food particles. The pump like action

and roughened surface of the tongue, and tiny hair-like projections (*lamellae*) on the inside of the beak aid the filtration process.

Greater flamingos are omnivores and feed on aquatic plants, worms, insect larvae, small molluscs, crustaceans and blue-green algae.

Lesser flamingos are herbivores and feed on aquatic plants and blue-green algae on the water surface.

Flamingos drink fresh water.

Communication

Flamingos are noisy and communicate with each other by making grunting, growling, honking sounds.

Reproduction

Flamingos are monogamous and only breed in the presence of large numbers. Mating is initiated by a spectacular courtship ritual that involves a lot of marching to and fro, standing tall and erect, stretching their necks in an upward direction, flapping their wings and repeated head turning, before they eventually pair off. A volcanic-shaped nest of mud, stones and feathers is built by both birds on the salt lake deposits. The nest can be as high as 30cm and takes six weeks to complete.

The female lays a single chalky coloured egg that is guarded and incubated by both parents for a period of up to 31 days. The chicks are a grey-white colour, and have a straight red bill, their eyes are initially grey but turn a yellow-orange colour by the time they are one year old. The short, stocky legs are a pink-red colour. Both parents are able to recognise their chick's call and feed it on crop milk until it is two months old. Crop milk has a high fat and protein content, it is dark red in colour and is produced by glands in the upper digestive tract. When the chick

is seven days old it will fledge and join a crèche watched over by other adults/babysitters while its parents go in search of food. The chicks are able to walk about on the salt flats, however if thickened salt-like deposits form around the chicks' ankles it makes it difficult or impossible for them to walk about and condemns them, with time, to a certain death.

By the time the chick is two to three months old its beak is sufficiently developed to allow it to filter food. As soon as the chicks are big enough they are taken by the adults on to the lake to be taught how to swim. They are able to fly by the time they are four months old, and by the time they are three years old they have taken on the adult pink colouration.

Flamingos reach sexual maturity between the ages of three and five years old. They begin to breed when they are six years old.

Predators/Threats

Flamingos are defenceless, and when threatened they will fly away. They have few natural predators due primarily to the remote, hostile, inhospitable environments in which they live. Their main predators are other birds such as marabou storks and African fish eagles, wildcats, and the occasional python. The eggs and chicks are preyed upon by the marabou stork and vultures. The marabou stork is particularly cruel and will kill the chicks without actually feeding on them. The main threat to the flamingo's survival is loss of habitat and polluted water.

Trivia

♦A combination of strong, intense sunlight, high temperatures, flamingo droppings, alkaline water and plankton encourage the growth and formation of the algae responsible for the unique pink colouration of the flamingo.

♦The colour of the flamingo is a good indicator of its health. A pale flamingo is under nourished and unhealthy, whereas a vibrantly coloured flamingo is well nourished and in good health.

♦The flamingo is nicknamed the flame bird.

♦The legs of the adult flamingo are longer than the body.

♦The brain of the flamingo is smaller than its eye.

♦Flamingos are able to drink water that is close to boiling point.

♦Salt is excreted from salt glands situated in the nostrils.

Marabou Stork
(*Leptoptilos crumeniferus*)
Swahili: *Batamaji*

Identification

The marabou stork is an extremely large wading bird and is one of the world's largest land birds that is able to fly.

Both sexes have a black plumage. White plumage is present behind the head, on the chest and belly and as tail feathers.

The head is bald with a sparse covering of downy feathers that extend as far as the nape of the neck. The skin on the head and neck is a pink-purple-red colour and is covered with irregular red-black spots. A large, pendulous reddish-pink throat wattle hangs down from its neck and is used in courtship rituals. The eyes are a greyish-brown colour. The beak is large, pointed and conical.

The bones of the legs and toes are hollow and the skin is naturally black although it usually appears to be white because the marabou stork regularly defecates down its legs, (this is believed to help regulate its body temperature as well as having strong antiseptic properties).

Males are taller and larger than females.

Height:	1.5m
Wing Span:	2.6m
Weight:	9kg

Habitat

Marabou storks are usually found in savannahs, grasslands and marsh land, near rivers, fishponds and lakes. They can also live close to human habitation in the vicinity of rubbish dumps and slaughterhouses.

Behaviour

Marabou storks are lazy, slow-moving birds that spend a lot of time standing still. They can have a solitary existence but usually live and breed in colonies alongside ibises, egrets, pelicans and storks and their numbers can range from 20 to 1000s. They are aggressive eaters, often found alongside vultures and hyenas feasting on carrion. In the presence of a grass fire they will wait at the edge of the blaze hoping to capture fleeing prey.

When in flight they keep their legs extended but retract their necks and they have the ability to soar at high altitude above the African plains.

Diet
Marabou storks are scavengers feeding on carrion, scraps from refuse heaps and slaughterhouses, small birds and mammals, reptiles, eggs, nestlings, amphibians, fish and insects. Indigestible food is regurgitated.

Marabou storks are able to access food more easily during the dry season as animals congregate in high concentration around dwindling water supplies.

Communication
Marabou storks are usually quiet, only making croaking noises or engaging in bill rattling during the mating season. When threatened they will emit a noise called beak clacking.

Reproduction
Marabou storks mate for life, and breed during the dry season. Their nests are made from twigs and are situated on treetops or ledges. The nest is never left unattended as other marabou storks will steal the twigs for their own nests. The nest is shallow and the centre is lined with smaller sticks and greenery. The female lays between two to five chalky-white eggs that are incubated for up to 31 days.

Both parents share the responsibility of incubating the eggs, feeding the young regurgitated food and teaching them how to fly and hunt.

The chick's down is short and white and is replaced after eight days with a second coat that is the same colour. They achieve the full adult black plumage between the ages of three to four years old.

The chicks make a lot of noise, croaking, whistling, whining and clattering. They are able to fly when they are two months old and are fully fledged by the time they are three to four months old, after which they break any maternal bonds that they have with their parents.

Marabou storks reach sexual maturity when they are four years old.

Predators/Threats

Marabou storks are preyed upon by the larger predators.

Trivia

♦The marabou stork is nick-named the undertaker bird due to its shape — it has cloak-like wings and skinny legs.

♦The marabou stork is the only species of stork to feed on carrion, they will also eat faeces.

♦Scavengers such as marabou storks usually have bald heads. When they are actively engaged in devouring a carcass their head will be covered in blood, other bodily fluids and matter that would be difficult to clean and be a source of infection if they were covered in feathers.

♦The feathers and down of the marabou stork are used to trim clothing and hats.

♦Marabou storks are sometimes considered to be a pest, but they do a marvellous job cleaning up carcasses that may be a source of disease.

♦Marabou storks can become tame when living close to human habitation.

Ostrich
(Struthio camelus)
Swahili: *Mbuni*

Identification

The ostrich is the largest and heaviest land bird in the world. It is also the fastest animal on two legs.

The male's plumage is black with the tips of the wings and tail feathers coloured white. The female's plumage is a dusty brown-grey colour. Between 50-60 tail feathers are present. The plumage is soft and has strong insulating properties. Ostriches are able to tolerate extreme variations in temperature.

The ostrich is a flightless bird. Strong stiffened wing and tail feathers required for flight are absent. Its wings are extremely short but very strong. Two claws are present on the tips of the wing fingers and are used in self defence.

The ostrich's head, long narrow neck and legs are bald, with a sparse covering of down. The skin on the female's neck and legs is tinged a pink-grey colour, whereas the male's is a grey-blue colour. The eyes are large and coloured brown, and are protected from the elements by long eyelashes. The broad, flattened pink beak has a rounded tip.

The legs are long and powerful with two toes on each foot. A sharp claw is present on the inner toe and assists in self defence and running. The ostrich can run at speeds of up to 70km/h and is able to maintain a constant speed of 50km/h when required.

The ostrich has excellent eyesight and hearing.

Height	Male 1.8-2.7m
	Female 1.7-2m
Wing Span:	2m
Weight:	100-155kg

Life Span
Up to 50 years in the wild.

Habitat

Ostriches are usually found in dry grasslands, savannahs, semi-deserts and desert areas.

Behaviour

Ostriches are nomadic, travelling alongside other grazers in the constant search of food, although males are territorial. They either live alone or in pairs, but during the mating season they may live in herds of between 5-50 individuals, led by a top hen.

In the presence of predators ostriches will either lie flat on the ground with their necks outstretched, appearing as a mound of earth on the ground, or they will run away. They are capable of outrunning any of the predators such as leopards, hyenas and lions. When threatened, the ostrich can deliver a single powerful blow with its legs that is capable of disembowelling and killing any predator.

Ostriches are diurnal and are most active early morning and late afternoon.

Diet

The ostrich is omnivorous, feeding primarily on grasses, shrubs, shoots, fruit, seeds, leaves, and nuts, supplementing its diet with invertebrates, (locusts, grasshoppers), and vertebrates, (small birds, lizards, frogs). Small stones and sand are swallowed to aid digestion. The ostrich requires very little water and is able to extract sufficient moisture from the plants it feeds on to meet its needs.

Communication

Ostriches use a variety of vocalisations to communicate with each other from whistling, hissing, growling, grunting and snorting to a low booming sound that it emits during the mating season. Bodily postures are used to intimidate rivals and warn off any predators.

Reproduction

Ostriches are polygamous and iteroparous. Mating commences between the months of March to April and ceases by September. The males (roosters) fight to win over a harem of between two to six females (hens). The dominant male (alpha male) initiates the mating process with an elaborate courtship ritual. He makes a lot of hissing noises, beats his wings repeatedly and pokes the ground with his beak to attract a female, before proceeding to mate. The male mates with all of the females but will only form a pair bond with the dominant female.

Ostriches are oviparous and lay their eggs in a communal nest over a three week period. The nest is constructed by the male, who scratches and scrapes the ground to create a hollow that is up to three metres in diameter and 30-60cm deep. The dominant female, who is able to recognise her own eggs, lays her eggs first in the centre of the nest and these are surrounded by eggs laid by the other females. Eggs on the periphery that are surplus to requirements are discarded. The eggs are a creamy-yellow colour and the surface of the shell is pitted. There will be between 15-60 eggs in the nest. These are incubated for up to 45 days by the dominant female during the day and by the male during the night.

When the chicks are ready to hatch, they call to their parents from inside the egg. Within minutes of been hatched the chicks are able to run around. Both parents play an active role in providing the chicks with food, water, shelter and shade, as well as protecting and defending them from predators. Growth is rapid and the chicks are independent by the time they are one year old.

Ostriches reach sexual maturity between two to four years old.

Predators/Threats

Ostriches are hunted by humans for their feathers, meat and skin, and when they are perceived by locals to be in competition with domestic livestock for grass. The feathers are used as feather dusters and are also used in the clothing industry. The meat, which tastes like beef, is low in cholesterol. The skin is used for leather goods. The fat and bone marrow are used in traditional medicines to treat conditions such as arthritis and rheumatism. The eggs are used to make jewellery and receptacles for carrying water. The young are preyed upon by hyenas, jackals and vultures.

Trivia

♦An ostrich is only able to kick forwards.

♦The ostrich's eyes are up to 5cm in diameter and are the largest of all known birds.

♦The ostrich is fond of water and likes to bathe in it.

♦The ostrich lays the largest eggs in the world, they are 18-23cm long, 11-15cm wide and weigh 1.3kg.

♦It takes a large pan and two hours to cook an ostrich egg to perfection.

♦Ostriches are bred commercially in some parts of the world for their meat, feathers and skin.

♦Ostriches are able to secrete urine separately from their faeces - an unusual trait for a bird.

Vulture
Swahili: *Tai*

Identification
Vultures are found in every continent in the world apart from Antarctica and Australia.

Vultures are medium to large-sized birds and are unique in that they scavenge for food and do not hunt and kill like other birds of prey. They fall into one of two group classifications:

New World Vultures:
There are seven species of New World vulture and they belong to the family Cathartdae. They are closely related to ibises and storks and are found in North, Central and South America.

Old World Vultures:
There are 15 species of Old World vulture and they belong to the family Accipitridae. They are closely related to buzzards, eagles, hawks and kites and are found in Africa, Asia and Europe.

Old World vultures are characterised by their bald head, short neck, long, broad, powerful wings and rounded tail. The beak is strong, sharp and hooked and assists in stripping the flesh from a carcass. They have excellent eyesight that has evolved with time, and the centre of the eye has a magnifying area that allows the vulture to accurately locate food. The ear is protected by a fine layer of skin that prevents blood and other bodily matter collecting in it when its head is inside a dead animal during feeding. The feet are strong with sharp talons. A back claw called a hallux is present, and this acts like a thumb enabling the vulture to manipulate objects.

Both male and female are a similar size and colour (black-brown), and are hard to distinguish from each other.

Length: 1m
Wingspan: 1.5-3.7m

Habitat
The vulture's dependence on its eyesight for locating food has restricted the habitat in which it is able to survive. They are usually

found in open countryside such as savannahs, semi-arid and desert areas.

Diet

Vultures are opportunistic, carnivorous scavengers that feed on carrion. Soaring high in the sky on warm thermals they spend many hours a day scanning the surrounding countryside, searching for food. Once food is located they land en masse. Food can be stored in a pouch in the throat called a crop, and is digested at a later time or regurgitated for the chicks. Strong, corrosive digestive juices enable the vulture to feed on carcasses that are in the advance stages of decay and contaminated with deadly bacteria that other animals are unable to tolerate (hog cholera, anthrax, and botulinum toxin). Never knowing when they will eat again they gorge themselves in a frenzied, chaotic feeding session.

After feeding, a lot of grooming and preening takes place before they retreat to a nearby tree to recover and digest their food.

Communication

Vultures are sociable yet shy, and are usually quiet, apart from when they are feeding.

Reproduction

Vultures are monogamous. The male initially attracts the attention of the female with a display of his flying skills before they pair off. The nest is made of leaves, twigs and sticks, high up in the hollow of a tree or on a cliff, and may be used for several years. Up to two eggs can be laid and both parents share the responsibility of incubating, feeding the young regurgitated food and teaching them how to hunt and fly. The incubation period is up to 50 days. When food is scarce, if two chicks are present the larger chick will kill the smaller one. The chicks are able to fly by the time they are three to six months old, until then they are relatively docile.

Predators/Threats

Because vultures are perceived as being aggressive, ugly, ungainly and cumbersome creatures, associated with scavenging on carrion, they are often misunderstood and persecuted by humans. Their breeding grounds and nests are destroyed, and they are killed for body parts to be used in witchcraft and sorcery. Poisoned bait is put out with the potential to kill many vultures at one time because of the large numbers present during feeding frenzies. As a result the vulture population can decline faster than any other species. What many people do not realise is that the vulture has an invaluable role to play in ridding the environment of dead, decaying and diseased animals, especially in hot climates. Lack of food and loss of habitat is also a threat to their survival.

Trivia

♦There are eight species of Old World vultures in Africa.

♦Scavengers such as vultures usually have bald heads. When they are actively engaged in devouring a carcass their head will be covered in blood, other bodily fluids and matter that would be difficult to clean and be a source of infection if they were covered in feathers.

♦It is extremely rare for a vulture to kill a live animal. If food is scarce, they may attack a newborn, or a sick, wounded animal.

♦Contrary to popular opinion vultures are not aggressive birds.

♦Old World vultures do not have a sense of smell.

♦Old World vultures roost during the night as their nighttime vision is poor.

♦Projectile corrosive vomit can be used as a deterrent when threatened.

♦Vultures urinate down their legs as the uric acid present in their urine kills bacteria and acts as a coolant.

♦A group of vultures on the ground is called a wake, committee or venue. When circling in the air a group of vultures is called a kettle.

♦Vultures are able to reduce a small mammal down to its skeleton in less than 30 minutes.

♦Contrary to popular opinion circling vultures are not necessarily an indication of the presence of dead prey on the ground, they may actually be enjoying soaring on hot thermals.

Agama
(*Agama agama*)
Swahili: *Mjusi kafiri*

Identification
Agamas are agile, small- to medium-sized, non-poisonous lizards native to Africa, Asia and Europe.

The agama has a large triangular-shaped head, with large eyes that have rounded pupils, and ears surrounded by clusters of spines. It has sharp, incisor-like teeth, with two fangs present in the upper jaw and a sticky tongue suited to catching prey. The body is covered in small scales, and long toes are present on all four limbs. The tail is long.

The agama's skin colour varies from a green-grey-brown colour to bright blue, pink or red, and they are consequently nicknamed "rainbow lizards". Some may have a stripe present down the centre of the back. The underside is a whitish colour. Males are always more brightly coloured than females.

Depending on species the length of the agama ranges from 12-38cm.

Habitat
Agamas are terrestrial and arboreal and are usually found in rocky outcrops, hillsides and semi-desert areas. They live and hide in rocks or the thatched roofs of mud huts, emerging to feed on prey.

Behaviour
Agamas are docile by nature and live in small groups of 10 to 20 individuals. Several females are present in the group alongside sub males who are led by a highly territorial dominant male (cock). Agamas do a lot of head nodding and head bobbing.

Frequent bouts of fighting occur when the dominant male is challenged by a subordinate or if a male wanders into its territory. The dominant male may change colour, do a lot of bobbing about, lash out with its tail and open its jaws wide to intimidate and confuse any rival. Agamas will run on their hind legs when threatened.

Agamas are diurnal.

Diet

The agama is primarily an insectivore and feeds primarily on ants, grasshoppers, beetles and termites, but will also eat grass, berries, seeds and the eggs of small lizards.

Reproduction

Agamas are polygamous and mate between March and May. During the mating season the male may change colour and will do a lot of head bobbing to attract and impress a female. Agamas are oviparous. The female lays between 7-18 eggs in a warm, damp, sandy, shallow hollow about 5cm deep. The eggs are laid between June and September and have an incubation period of eight to ten weeks.

Female are sexually mature between 14-18 months old.

Males are sexually mature at two years old.

Predators/Threats

Agamas are natural prey for snakes.

Chameleon
(*Chamaeleonidae*)
Swahili: *Kinyonga*

Identification

Chameleons are small to medium-sized arboreal lizards. There are between 80-150 different species and they are native to India, Sri Lanka, Spain, Madagascar and other areas of Africa.

The head is triangular with a pointed crest. Depending on species, horns and spines may be present. The eyes are tiny and situated on a large, conical protrusion. A small ,yellow ring surrounds a black eye. The eyes are able to rotate, and move independently of each other, but will face forwards when focused on prey. External ears are absent.

The chameleon has a long, sticky, elastic, prehensile tongue that curls up inside its mouth. The tongue can actually be the full length of its body, it is fast moving and is used to catch prey. Teeth are present on the lower jaw.

The body is flattened laterally. It has a long prehensile tail that wraps itself around the tree branches so to help maintain balance.

The legs are long and slender. Five toes are present on all four limbs and are fused together in bundles of two or three, this affords the chameleon a pincer-like grip with which to hold onto the branches of trees as it slowly rocks forwards. Sharp claws are present on each toe.

The dry, rough skin has varying shades of green-grey-brown. The colour of the skin changes involuntarily, and is stimulated by

temperature, light and emotion. Hot temperatures, bright lights and anger darkens the colour of the skin. Cold temperatures, darkness and excitement or fear lightens the colour of the skin.

The chameleon has excellent eyesight.

Body Length: 2.5-68cm depending on species.

Habitat
Chameleons mostly live in trees and bushes, and are found in tropical and mountainous rain forests, woodlands, savannahs, semi-deserts and deserts. Some species live on the ground.

Diet
Chameleons are insectivores and feed on locusts, flies, mosquitoes, crickets, beetles and grass hoppers. Larger species may eat small birds.

Reproduction
Chameleons may be oviparous or ovoviviparous. The gestation period, incubation period and number of eggs laid varies from species to species.

Predators/Threats
Snakes (boomslangs and vine snakes in particular) are the main natural predators of the chameleon, followed closely by birds. Garden and agricultural pesticides either poison the chameleon or they starve to death because of the lack of food. Grass fires quickly destroy their habitat.

Monitor Lizard
(*Varanidae*)
Swahili: *Kenge*

Identification
Monitor lizards are large reptiles found in the tropical and sub-tropical regions of Africa, Asia and Australia. They are usually found in deserts, forests or grasslands.

The monitor lizard has a long flexible neck, a small head and large, powerful jaws that enable it to swallow large prey. Its flickering forked tongue is used to sniff the air and collect airborne particles to pass onto sensory tissue in the Jacobson's Organ which is in the roof of the mouth. This tells the monitor lizard all it needs to know about prospective prey, the presence of predators and the environment. The monitor lizard's body is large and heavy with four short, strong legs equipped with long powerful claws. The tail is long and powerful. Despite its cumbersome appearance the monitor lizard is surprisingly agile and is able to climb, swim and burrow with ease. Depending on species the body length ranges from 20cm to 3m, and an individual may weigh up to 165kg. Some monitor lizards, such as the Komodo, are venomous.

Habitat
The majority of monitor lizards are terrestrial, some are arboreal and others semi-aquatic or aquatic.

Behaviour
By nature monitor lizards are aggressive, ill-tempered and hostile. They will avoid confrontation where possible and seek flight, but where there is no alternative they will use bodily postures, hiss a lot, enlarge their throat and expand their ribs while lashing out wildly with the tail to ward off any predators.

Monitor lizards are diurnal.

Diet
Monitor lizards are carnivorous and feed on birds, small mammals, crayfish, eggs, frogs, turtles, snakes, crocodile hatchlings and

invertebrates. Close to human habitation they will feed on domestic livestock (cats, dogs, pigs, goats, chickens) as well as carrion.

Reproduction
Monitor lizards are oviparous and lay a clutch between 2-60 eggs, either in a burrow in the ground or in the hollow of a tree. The eggs incubate for a period of 56-70 days. The young use an egg tooth to break the shell.

Trivia
♦The monitor lizard is unable to grow its tail back if it loses it.

♦The bacteria in the mouth of the monitor lizard is highly toxic and can be fatal to the victim if bitten.

Nile Crocodile
(*Crocodylus niloticus*)
Swahili: *Mamba*

Identification

The crocodile is a large, amphibious, lizard-like reptile. It has a long, streamlined body and tail, with four short legs equipped with sharp claws. There are five toes on the forelegs that are suited to digging in the sand, and four webbed toes on the hind legs that assist with swimming.

The head is large with a broad, elongated, tapering snout. The eyes, ears and nostrils are placed high on the crocodile's flattened head, allowing it to see, hear, and smell above the surface of the water when it is submerged. The tiny eyes are green and the pupils are vertical. A third eyelid protects the eyes under water.

The jaws are strong and powerful, and the long, conical teeth, which can number up to 66, are designed to endure the stresses and strains of firmly holding on to struggling prey. The teeth interlock and are clearly visible when the crocodile's mouth is closed. The fourth tooth in particular, protrudes from the lower jaw and fits into a notch on the upper jaw. The teeth continue to grow throughout life.

The hide is thick, rough and scaly. Rows of ossified, overlapping raised horny scales (*scutes*) run the length of the back and tail. The scutes offer camouflage, protection and help control body temperature. A fine mesh of blood vessels runs up and down through the scutes to the surface, absorbing energy from the sun, which increases the crocodile's body temperature.

Juveniles are dark brown/olive green in colour with dark crossbands on the body and tail. The adults are darker with crossbands that fade as they age. The underbelly has smooth scales that are a yellow-grey colour.

Crocodiles have excellent eyesight, hearing and sense of smell.

Male crocodiles are 30% larger than the female.

Nose to Tail Length:	Male	3.5-5m
	Female	4m
Weight:	Male	500-550kg
	Female	300-350kg

NB: Large males can be up to 1,000kg

135

Life Span
Forty-five years in the wild.

Habitat
Crocodiles are found in waterholes, ponds, lakes, rivers, estuaries, freshwater marshes and swamps. They usually remain in the same territory throughout their natural lives, only moving when drought conditions cause the water to dry up.

Behaviour
Crocodiles are sociable animals and usually live in a small group called a bask.

Both the male (bull) and female (cow) are territorial, especially during the mating season. They do not like intruders and defend their territories aggressively.

Crocodiles are cold-blooded creatures. They are inactive when cool, and active when warm. They spend a considerable amount of time during the day on the banks of the river, sliding up onto the banks on their bellies to bask in the sun, usually with their mouths wide open, venting off heat. They return to the water when they need to cool down, or when they are startled. Crocodiles can lift their bellies up off the ground and high walk. They can run at speeds of 17km/h over short distances, but tire quickly. Small crocodiles can bound like a rabbit.

The crocodile is the ultimate predator, highly skilled, effective and opportunistic, either hunting on its own or as part of a team. Moving with ease through the water they can swim at 32km/h. They lie in wait, submerged beneath the water, waiting for the unsuspecting prey to approach the water's edge, before launching a speedy, surprise attack.

Locking their powerful jaws on to the prey they drag it underwater. They then spin the body round to disorientate and drown the prey. This is known as the crocodile death roll. Crocodiles are unable to chew, so by spinning the body in the water they are able to tear off chunks of flesh, which they swallow whole. The crocodile has two aortas. The additional aorta saturates the blood in carbon dioxide—a vital ingredient for the production of stomach acid, which is necessary for the digestion of the massive prey they hunt.

Crocodiles are nocturnal, but can be observed basking in the sun during the day.

Diet

The crocodile is carnivorous, capable of eating half of its body weight. The majority (70%) of the crocodile's diet is made up from large fish. It will eat any animals, including humans, that come its way—warthogs, antelopes, zebras, buffalo, wildebeest, hippos, porcupines, large cats, reptiles and carrion. If the crocodile's body temperature falls below 24°C it loses its appetite and ability to digest food.

The crocodile swallows small stones to aid digestion and can survive long periods without eating.

Juveniles feed on insects, frogs and small reptiles.

Reproduction

Crocodiles are polygamous, mating in the dry season with the young hatching in the wet season.

Mating takes place in water and is a noisy affair; the male (bull) attracts the female's attention by bellowing, expelling water out of both nostrils and slapping the surface of the water with its snout

The female lays between 25-100 eggs in November and December, in a nest that is 50cm deep, and several metres away from the water's edge. The eggs are left to incubate for 80-90 days. During this time, the male and female closely guard the nest, as they are frequently raided by hyenas, water mongoose, baboons, monkeys, monitor lizards and humans. When the hatchlings are ready to hatch, they call to their parents from inside the egg. A horn or egg tooth that is present on the tip of the snout helps to break the egg shell. Both parents assist the hatchling by gently cracking the egg shell open with their mouths. The female carries the hatchlings in her jaws to the water's edge.

If threatened, the female will protect the young by placing them

inside her mouth or on her back. The young crocodiles live in a family group until they are two years old. Monitor lizards, turtles, catfish, baboons, honey badgers, white tailed mongoose, marabou storks, herons, and ibises are the main threat to the survival of the young crocodile.

Females reach sexual maturity when they are 2.5m long and are usually ten years old. Males are sexually mature when they are 3-3.1m long and are also usually ten years old.

Communication
The crocodile is the most vocal of all the reptiles. It uses a variety of vocalisations to communicate when distressed, when mating, when patrolling its territory and when threatened. Visual signals, bodily postures, touch and scents are also used to communicate with each other.

Predators/Threats
The crocodile does not have any natural predators. They are hunted for their valuable hide and meat. They are in competition with local fishermen for food, and regularly get tangled up in their fishing nets from which they cannot escape, and death follows quickly from drowning.

Loss of habitat is the only other threat to the crocodile's survival.

Trivia
♦It is believed that crocodiles evolved from dinosaurs, and have inhabited the earth for over 240 million years.

♦Crocodiles do not shed their skin like other reptiles; instead they grow with it.

♦The crocodile is Africa's largest predator and is top of the food chain.

♦The crocodile has the most powerful bite in the animal kingdom.

♦The crocodile is able to close its nostrils underwater.

♦The temperature in the nest determines the sex of the crocodile.

♦Temperatures below 31.7°C or above 34.5°C produce females. Males are born in the narrow temperature range between 31.7°C and 34.5°C. Usually the eggs at the top of the nest are female and those lower down are male.

♦Crocodiles can remain underwater for 30 minutes when threatened. The diaphragm, which is attached to the ribs and the pubic bone (part of the hip bone), pulls the liver backwards and allows the pleural cavity to expand to increase the volume of air entering the lungs. The ability to increase or decrease its centre of buoyancy allows the crocodile to adjust its position in the water without making a ripple or splash.

♦Crocodiles do not have sweat glands. Keeping their mouths open while sleeping or basking on river banks helps to reduce their temperature.

♦Locals perceive crocodiles as being very dangerous, hostile creatures.

♦Crocodiles are immune to anthrax.

Snakes
Swahili: *Nyoka*

Snakes are found in every continent in the world apart from Antarctica, inhabiting a variety of environments that range from equatorial rain forests, tropical jungles and temperate forests to savannahs, grasslands deserts, swamps, seas and oceans.

Snakes are legless reptiles with long, narrow bodies. Depending on species, body length ranges from 13cm to 11m and weight from 1g to 226kg. The musculoskeletal system of snakes is made up of a skull and 130-500 vertebrae, with attached ribs. Flexible, elastic ligaments allow movement between the small bones of the skull, as well as allowing the upper and lower jaws to open as wide as 150°, enabling the snake to swallow large prey.

Their eyesight is poor, but they are sensitive to movement. A protective transparent cap (*brille*), covers the lidless eyes and restricts movement.

External ears are absent. A small bone in the ear (*columella*), detects vibration and the body is also sensitive to vibration.

Some snakes have specialised heat sensing organs present in the upper and lower jaws to detect warm-blooded prey. This is especially useful during the hours of darkness.

The snake's flickering, forked tongue is used to sniff the air and to collect airborne particles to pass on to sensory tissue in the Jacobson's Organ. The Jacobson's Organ is found in all vertebrates, it is located in the roof of the mouth and is well developed in reptiles, especially snakes. It tells the snake all it needs to know about its prospective prey or the presence of predators, as well as informing the male of the reproductive status of nearby females.

Despite its shiny, slimy appearance the skin of a snake is actually very dry. Numerous small, thin scales are present on the back and sides and help to protect it from abrasions and dehydration. The scales (*scutes*) on the underside are fewer in number and thicker, and they protect and support the tissues that are in direct contact with ground. Snakes frequently shed their skin as they outgrow it, and those that grow rapidly shed their skins more frequently. Before a snake sheds its skin it will go into hiding, this is due to the skin over the eyes becoming opaque and blurring its vision so it is particularly vulnerable to predators at this time.

The young shed their skin at least 50-60 times during their first year of life. The snake's scales, colour and unique patterns provide excellent camouflage from predators and prey alike.

Powerful muscles on the underside grip the ground surface to help propel the snake forwards. Snakes cannot move backwards.

Snakes are cold-blooded vertebrates and are most active at temperatures between 25-32°C. The high temperature in the tropics causes them to grow more rapidly than in cooler parts of the world. It is worth bearing in mind that the higher the temperature, the greater the risk of a chance meeting, and it is common to find snakes on roads and paths, especially at night, where the temperature is higher than in the surrounding bush.

Snakes are carnivorous. Depending on species they eat worms, small and large invertebrates, small mammals, birds, eggs, fish, reptiles and amphibians. They either kill their prey by constriction or by a venomous bite. When constricting prey, the snake coils itself round the victim and each time the victim breathes out the snake tightens its grip until the victim dies of asphyxiation or cardiac arrest.

Non-poisonous snakes, which are usually the constrictors, have two rows of teeth in the upper jaw and one row of teeth in the lower jaw. The teeth break easily but are quickly replaced. The teeth, which are short, sharp, and curved backwards towards the throat, prevent live prey from escaping. Snakes do not chew their food, they swallow their prey whole, regardless of whether it is dead or alive. Digestion of prey is assisted by powerful digestive enzymes. If disturbed or threatened shortly after eating, a snake will regurgitate its food so that it can escape.

Venomous snakes have one row of teeth in the upper jaw and have a pair of grooved-out fangs that the venom flows down, or hollowed-out fangs that the venom flows through. Hollowed-out fangs can either be fixed or folded. Folded fangs are located at the front of the mouth, they fold back into the mouth when closed, but open up when the mouth is open. Fangs inject venom into the prey from glands located at the back of the upper jaw or on top of the head. Fangs fall out several times a year and are then replaced. During the digestive process, the snake is relatively inactive. Plant matter, hair and claws are indigestible and are excreted. Snakes have a low metabolic rate so they do not need to continually eat large amounts of food.

Snakes live alone and only meet up to mate. This may be quite a tortuous process for the male, sometimes lasting many days before he succeeds. Depending on species the female either:

♦Lays soft-shelled eggs that hatch after a period of incubation (oviparous).

♦Gives birth to young that have developed in an egg inside the mother's body, which break free within minutes of being born (ovoviviparous).

♦Gives birth to live young (viviparous) that are independent from the moment they are born and are as deadly as their parents.

Snakes reach sexual maturity between nine months and up to three years old.

Snakes only bite when cornered, threatened, startled or provoked and such attacks are used as a means of defence or self preservation. Venomous snakes have the ability to decide whether or not to inject venom into the aggressor. They do not want to waste precious venom on unsuitable prey as it takes four days to three weeks to replenish. On such occasions they deliver a dry bite.

Snake venom is a deadly, toxic cocktail consisting of proteins, toxins and enzymes and it acts in one of four ways to subdue, immobilise and eventually kill its prey. It is either: haematoxic, cytotoxic, neurotoxic or cardiotoxic. In some species it can be a combination.

Effects of Snake Venom on Humans

Haematoxic Venom (Heart and Cardiovascular System)

The effects of haematoxic venom are immediately evident. There is severe pain, marked swelling and discolouration of the soft tissues at the site of the bite. Haematoxic venom affects the ability of the blood to clot, resulting in loss of blood from the body's external orifices, and eventual death from severe internal haemorrhaging and major organ failure.

A haematoxic bite is the most painful of all snake bites.

Cytotoxic Venom (Localised effect)

Cytotoxic toxic venom initially results in localised tissue damage. The body responds to the presence of venom in the soft tissues by sending plasma to the site of the bite in an attempt to dilute it. There is marked swelling and a reduction or loss of circulation to the body part,

142

which may precipitate gangrene. If this bite is not treated promptly it can result in amputation and eventual death.

A cytotoxic bite is extremely painful.

Neurotoxic Venom (Central Nervous System)

Neurotoxic venom is extremely fast acting and affects the central nervous system. The transmission of nerve impulses to muscles involved in swallowing, respiration, speech and sight are affected, and this results in paralysis. If untreated, death is inevitable and will occur between 20 minutes and 4 hours after the bite. The victim dies of cardiac or respiratory arrest.

A neurotoxic bite is not particularly painful. Symptoms are not always obvious and may appear some time later.

Cardiotoxic Venom

Cardiotoxic venom directly affects the heart and to leads to circulatory failure and shock.

Trivia

♦Snakes are unable to chew food because of the curvature of their teeth.

♦The hedgehog, mongoose, secretary bird and honey badger are immune to an ordinary, average dose of snake venom.

♦It is impossible to distinguish male and female snakes from each other as their markings and coloration are identical. They all look the same!

♦A snake that has hatched from an egg is known as a hatchling. A newly born snake is known as a neonate or snakelet.

♦Snakes continue to grow until they die.

♦Children are usually bitten by snakes when playing in the bush.

♦Adult humans are often bitten by snakes when they are working in the fields or when they have entered their homes during the night. In the rainy season (April to June), when the weather is cooler, puff adders and cobras are forced out of their burrows and will enter houses in search of warmth and food. Traditional dwellings such as mud huts provide easy access.

♦The majority of snake bites are to the lower leg, so when walking in the bush it is advisable to wear long trousers and leather boots that go above the ankle, this makes it more difficult for a snake bite to

143

actually penetrate the skin. Snakes rely on detecting movement, so if they are encountered in the bush it is best to stand still and wait for them to move on. The boomslang and twig snake are able to see and recognise stationary objects as prey.

♦Snake venom has been used medicinally for thousands of years by the ancient Egyptians, and as an aphrodisiac by the Chinese. Modern medicine is currently researching the possible benefits of snake venom in the treatment of cancer and high blood pressure.

♦The major threat to the snake's survival is loss of habitat. They are hunted by humans for their skin and meat.

♦Snakes can climb up beneath stationary cars and travel hundreds of miles without detection. If you do suspect that a snake has crawled under your vehicle, it needs to be flushed out using a long stick such as a walking pole or tent pole.

♦Snakes are the most feared animal among local people in some parts of East Africa.

Estivation

Estivation is similar to hibernation and is a period of dormancy, but takes place when temperatures are high and the weather is dry. Invertebrates or vertebrates that estivate do so because they are unable to tolerate high temperatures and need to find a safe, cool place to rest in, usually underground. During this period their bodily functions slow down, and they do not move or grow.

African Rock Python
(*Python sebae*)
Swahili: *Chatu*

Identification

The African rock python is the largest snake in Africa and the third largest snake in the world. It is potentially a very dangerous snake to encounter—its strength, and the speed at which it can strike should never be under estimated.

The background colour of the python's skin is light brown/tan to grey brown, on which there are numerous irregular, light brown to olive green transverse blotches outlined in black. The underside is a creamy white colour. There are two dark bands on the tip of the tail.

The python has a triangular head. A tan, V-shaped band extends from the snout to just above each eye.

The absence of a breast bone, combined with flexible ligaments that allow the upper and lower jaw to open wide, enables the python to swallow large prey. The python is non venomous and does not possess fangs. Its teeth are short, sharp and curved backwards towards the throat, preventing prey, if still alive, from escaping.

Length: Males 7-8m
Females 4-6m
Weight: 45-90kg

Habitat

Pythons are found in savannahs, woodlands, forests and grasslands at altitudes of up to 2,300m. They live alone in rocky outcrops, deserted termite mounds and underground animal burrows. Dependent on water, they are found in close proximity to lakes, rivers, streams and swamps. Pythons are terrestrial but can climb trees if required.

Juveniles live in drier areas but as they mature they move towards water.

Behaviour

Pythons are solitary, bad-tempered, vicious and unpredictable. Easily provoked, when threatened or harassed they are capable of delivering a swift, painful bite before constricting their victim.

The python is an opportunistic predator that hunts alone at twilight. Heat-sensing organs present in the upper and lower jaws, and sensory tissue in the Jacobson's Organ enable the python to detect warm-blooded prey, and compensate for its poor eyesight. Stalking its victim patiently, it strikes with astonishing speed. Wrapping its coils round the victim, the python tightens its grips with each exhalation, until the victim dies of asphyxiation or cardiac arrest. It swallows its prey head first and whole. Strong acids in the stomach digest the prey. While digesting its food the python is vulnerable to predators, such as hyenas and wild dogs. After eating a large animal the python does not need to eat for a long period of time—in some instances this may be as long as a year.

Pythons are dependent on water in which to cool down and are fast swimmers. They are able to remain submerged for long periods when hunting prey in water.

Pythons are nocturnal, occasionally basking in the mid day sun. They estivate (hibernate) during the dry season when temperatures are high, taking refuge in deserted, underground animal burrows. They eat well before they estivate, usually selecting medium-sized mammals such as antelopes.

Juveniles are active at dawn and dusk.

Diet
Pythons are carnivorous and feed on small- to medium-sized mammals (hyrax, hares, antelopes, monkeys, goats, gazelles), fish, lizards, birds, livestock and, very rarely, humans.

Juveniles feed on small mammals such as rats.

Reproduction
Pythons are only seen together during the mating season between November and March, during which time they do not eat. Pythons are oviparous (lay eggs). Three months after mating the female lays between 20-100 eggs in a tree hollow, deserted termite mound or underground animal burrow. Coiling herself around the eggs, keeping them warm and safe from predators (monitor lizards, mongoose), she only leaves them for a short period of time to drink water. Throughout this period the female continues to fast until the eggs hatch. The incubation period is between 60-80 days.

The young (hatchlings) are independent at birth, have identical markings to the adults, but are more striking and vibrantly coloured. The female remains with the young for another two weeks, or until they have shed their first skin.

Females reach sexual maturity between three and five years old and mate when they are 2.7m long.

Males reach sexual maturity between three and five years old and mate when they are 2.1m long.

Predators/Threats

Adult pythons do not have any natural predators. They are hunted for their skin, meat and fat. Small pythons are hunted by monitor lizards, crocodiles, birds of prey, badgers, mongooses, cats and pigs.

Trivia

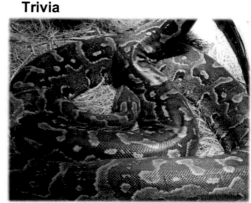

♦Pythons continue to grow all of their lives. The more they eat, the faster they grow and the bigger they get.

♦Although terrestrial, pythons can be found resting in acacia trees in swampy areas such as in Tarangire National Park and Lake Nakuru National Park.

♦Pythons are good at pest control, as they keep the number of rodents down.

♦Pythons have been known to constrict and consume humans, although this is extremely rare.

Black Mamba
(Dendroaspis polylepis)
Swahili: *Koboko mweusi*

Identification
The black mamba is the largest and deadliest venomous snake in the African continent. It is the fastest moving land snake, capable of speeds of 20km/h.

The black mamba is a large, streamlined snake. Its skin is dark, and is either grey, olive green or brown coloured. The underside is lighter, and is either creamy, or a pale olive green colour. The colour of their skin darkens with age.

The black mamba's face is paler than the body and the eyes are either green, brown or black. The inside of the mouth is black. It has two long, hollow, fixed, venomous fangs.

Length: 2.4-3m

Habitat
Black mambas are usually found in savannahs, grasslands, open wood lands and semi-arid deserts below 1,500m. They live in rocky outcrops, tree hollows, deserted termite mounds and underground animal burrows. Black mambas are terrestrial but can climb trees if necessary.

Behaviour
Dangerous, easily angered and aggressive when threatened, the black mamba is highly unpredictable under these circumstances. Normally the black mamba will avoid confrontation and will quietly slither away. However when cornered it will hiss repeatedly as a warning, expand a narrow cobra-like hood near its neck, flick its tongue and raise its body by up to one third from the ground. Movement causes the mamba to strike, which is why potential human victims are usually advised to keep perfectly still. The black mamba strikes and delivers its deadly poison with incredible precision, and is capable of up to 12 multiple strikes. The venom is neuro- and cardio-toxic.

A bold, aggressive hunter, the black mamba identifies, and then patiently and silently stalks its prey. When the opportunity arises, it will strike its prey once or twice, and then allow it to wander off to die. Death is usually swift, after which the prey is swallowed whole.

The black mamba lives in a permanent lair. A creature of habit, if left undisturbed it will occupy the same lair for many years. It also has regular, daily basking spots.

The black mamba is diurnal.

Diet
Black mambas are carnivorous and feed on small mammals (voles, rats, mice, hyraxes, squirrels and bush babies), reptiles and the occasional bird.

Reproduction
Black mambas mate once a year in the spring and lay their eggs in the summer.

The male black mamba locates the female by following her scent trail, and after inspecting her entire body with his flickering tongue, their bodies intertwine and they begin the long, drawn out mating process. They part company shortly afterwards and return to their lairs.

Black mambas are oviparous. The female waits up to 60 days before laying 10-25 eggs in a warm, damp burrow after which she abandons them. The young use an egg tooth to break the shell open between two to three months after incubation. They are independent from the moment they are born and are as deadly as their parents. Growth is rapid.

Black mambas reach sexual maturity when they are 0.9-1.2m long.

Predators/Threats
Adult black mambas have few predators. Their deadly venom makes them a formidable proposition for any potential predator. They may be killed by the secretary bird or birds of prey, and out of fear, by humans. The main threat to their survival is loss of habitat. The eggs

and the young are subject to predation by birds of prey, mongooses, crocodiles, monitor lizards, foxes and jackals.

Trivia

♦The black mamba is the second largest venomous snake in the world after the King Cobra.

♦Local people call the black mamba the "seven step snake", as that is as far as you will be able to walk after you have been bitten before feeling the effects of the deadly venom.

♦A bite from the black mamba is known as the kiss of death. Before the development of anti-venom, a bite from a black mamba was 100% fatal, with the victim dying within 20 minutes to 4 hours later. Other snakes' venom can take several days to take effect and kill the victim.

♦The venom of the black mamba is yellow in colour.

♦The faeces of the black mamba smell of curry powder.

♦Black mambas are often considered to be good pest controllers as they help to keep the number of rodents down.

Boomslang
(Dispholidus typus)
Swahili: *Kijoka mti/Kimkufu*

Identification

The boomslang is a highly venomous, agile and fast-moving snake.

The boomslang is long slender snake. Females are usually a brown-olive colour. Males are more brightly coloured than females and are usually black, brown or green. Juveniles are darker with a distinct, lighter underside.

Its most distinguishing features are the disproportionately enormous eyes with rounded pupils, pointed snout and relatively small, egg-shaped head.

It has large grooved, fangs located at the back of the mouth and is able to open its jaws to 170° allowing it to bite large objects such as a human leg or arm.

The boomslang has good eyesight.

Length: 1-1.5m

Habitat

Boomslangs are usually found in savannahs, grasslands and woodlands. It is arboreal and lives in trees, bushes and shrubs, occasionally hunting prey at ground level.

Behaviour

The boomslang is a good-natured, placid, timid snake that is well camouflaged and rarely seen. If startled, threatened or provoked the boomslang will inflate its neck to double its size and will strike instantly.

Boomslangs are diurnal.

Diet

Boomslangs are carnivorous and feed on small mammals, chameleons, lizards, frogs, birds and birds' eggs.

Reproduction

Boomslangs are oviparous. The female lays between 8-25 eggs in the late spring to mid-summer, either in a tree hollow or on a mound of leaves. The incubation period is between 70-100 days. The hatchlings are initially a greyish colour with blue specks, taking on adult colouration several years later.

Predators/Threats
Loss of habitat.

Trivia

◆The wide variations in the skin colour make it very difficult to identify the boomslang. This would be critical if you were bitten by a snake out in the bush. The boomslang's venomous bite is difficult to treat as it requires a specific anti-venom to be effective.

◆Boomslangs mate in the trees.

◆The boomslang has the widest variation of skin colour of all the African snakes.

◆Boomslangs hibernate for short periods in cool weather.

◆The venom of the boomslang is highly potent, slow acting and haemotoxic. ◆A bite from a boomslang is extremely rare, but must be taken seriously. Medical treatment should commence immediately, even though the individual feels well. Symptoms may take 24-48 hours to manifest, by which time it will be too late.

◆The venom of the boomslang is more toxic than the venom of the black mamba, but because it is delivered in a reduced quantity it takes longer to take effect on its victim.

Puff Adders
(Bitis arietans)
Swahili: *Kifutu*

Identification

Common and widely distributed, this dangerous and highly venomous snake is responsible for 60% of all fatalities in the African continent.

The puff adder is a large viper with a thickened body and shortened tail. The background colour of the puff adder's skin is yellow-orange to brown-grey. Black chevrons with pale outer edges run the full length of the back. The underside is a pale yellow-white colour, on which blotches may be present.

The puff adder has a large, broad, flat, triangular-shaped head with a blunt rounded snout and two large nostrils that point in an upwards direction. A dark V-shaped band extends from the snout to above each eye, and its pupils are vertical.

The teeth of the puff adder are extremely sharp, and two long, hollow, erectile fangs are situated at the front of the mouth.

Males are larger than females and have longer tails.

Length:	1m
Fang Length:	2cm
Weight:	4-6kg

Habitat

Puff adders are usually found in savannahs, grasslands and open woodlands, they have a particular liking for rocky outcrops. Puff adders are terrestrial, but can climb trees and swim if required.

Behaviour

Bad-tempered, lazy, slow-moving and well camouflaged, the puff adder makes no attempt to move out of the way when it can sense the vibrations from your footsteps as you travel towards it. Basking in the sun they are usually found on or close to footpaths and roads, and will not hesitate to strike if startled, provoked or accidently trodden on. When threatened they may attempt to retreat backwards towards cover, but usually they inflate their body with air, do a lot of hissing and puffing as a warning, and then strike. If required they can strike a second time. The long fangs enable the puff adder to deliver its lethal, cytotoxic venom deep into the soft tissues. The bite is extremely painful and produces extensive swelling and discolouration of the soft tissues within 10-30 minutes.

Puff adders use "wait and see" tactics to ambush their unsuspecting prey, which are usually rodents. After striking, they let go of their victim, and allow it to wander off to die before moving in to swallow it whole.

Puff adders are diurnal and nocturnal.

Diet
Puff adders are carnivorous and feed on small mammals (rats, mice and voles), amphibians, lizards, small snakes and birds.

Reproduction
Puff adders are viviparous. The gestation period is between 210-270 days with the female giving birth to 20-60 snakelets in the late summer. The young are as deadly as their parents, capable of delivering a venomous bite.

Predators/Threats
Puff adders have few predators. They may be killed by birds of prey, other snakes, badgers, warthogs and out of fear by humans. Loss of habitat, especially in coastal areas is a threat to their survival.

Trivia
♦The puff adder may act dead, but will strike back when it gets the opportunity. Its nervous system remains active for some time after death, during which time it is still able to bite.

♦The fangs of the puff adder are able to penetrate soft leather.

♦Puff adders are frequently found on roads and footpaths as these areas are warmer than the surrounding bush. Animals are also attracted to the footpaths, as they like to bask, walk, run and wallow about in open spaces. ♦Leaving traces of their fur, feathers and scent, these animals attract puff adders to the vicinity, with potentially deadly consequences.

♦Before the puff adder sheds its skin, there is a reduction in skin colour; after it has shed its skin, its original colour and vibrancy returns.

Other wildlife that you may come across

Bat-Eared Fox
(*Otocyon megalotis*)
Swahili: *Bweha masigio*

Identification
The bat-eared fox is a small African fox, that has a jackal-like appearance.

The body is small and slender with a long, grey-brown bushy coat and a paler underside. The tail is long and bushy with a black upper surface and tip.

The bat-eared fox has a small face with a broad forehead, enormous conspicuous ears and a short, pointed muzzle. The teeth, of which there are up to 50, are small and are suited to eating and grinding down insects. The face is black below the eye with white patches around the eyes and muzzle. The backs of the ears are black with lighter fur on the inside. Blood circulating thorough the capillaries in the ears is cooled, preventing the bat-eared fox from overheating.

The short, black, slender legs are equipped with powerful, non-retractable claws for digging. There are five toes on the forefoot and four toes on the hind foot.

The bat-eared fox has excellent hearing.

Head & Body Length:	46-60cm
Shoulder Height:	30-40cm
Tail:	30-35cm
Ears:	13-14cm
Weight:	3-5kg

Habitat
Bat-eared foxes are usually found in savannahs, grassland, lightly wooded areas and semi-deserts.

Behaviour
Bat-eared foxes are very shy and sociable and live in a small family group of up to six individuals. The family consists of the mated pair and their offspring, and they live together in a den, which is usually an

155

abandoned burrow. If the need arises they are capable of digging and making a den of their own underground. The den usually has several entrances and numerous, underground interconnecting tunnels. They occasionally scent mark their territory with urine.

Bat-eared foxes are agile and capable of running fast in a zigzag manner when pursued by predators before swiftly disappearing underground to the safety of their den.

Bat-eared foxes are primarily nocturnal. Emerging from their dens at dusk they will initially play together and groom each other before going to forage for food. Walking alone, slowly and quietly, with their ears cocked forwards and their noses to the ground, they listen intently for the underground movement of insects, stopping only to dig up prey when it is located. They may be active early morning and late afternoon, and will rest at midday.

Diet
Bat-eared foxes are omnivores, feeding primarily on termites, beetles, scorpions, centipedes, grasshoppers, ants, crickets and locusts, supplementing their diet with small birds and mammals, lizards, snakes, eggs and fruit. They are able to extract sufficient moisture from the food they eat.

Communication
A sociable animal, the bat-eared fox uses a variety of vocalisations (whistling), facial expressions (particularly the ears), and bodily and tail postures to communicate with other foxes.

Reproduction
Bat-eared foxes are monogamous and breed once a year. It is not unusual for a male (reynard) to live with two females (vixen) in a shared communal den. Both parents share the responsibility of caring, protecting, grooming and playing with the cubs.

The gestation period is between 60-70 days. The female gives birth to a litter of two to six cubs, usually at the start of the rainy season when there is an abundance of insects to feed on. Newborn cubs are a light grey colour and are born blind, with their eyes opening after nine days.

The female only has four nipples to suckle the cubs on. She actively kills some of the young to increase the remaining cubs' chances of survival.

The cubs emerge from the den when they are two to three weeks old and are looked after by the male while the female is out foraging for food—this is because she needs to maximise the amount of milk she produces as the cubs are not fed on regurgitated food. Weaning begins when they are one month old and is complete by the time they are 15 weeks old. The cubs reach adult size by the time they are six months old and may remain with their parents until they are one year old.

Sexual maturity is reached when bat-eared foxes are nine months old.

Predators/Threats

Bat-eared foxes are natural prey for African wild dogs, hyenas, cheetahs, lions, leopards, jackals, pythons and birds of prey. They are not a threat to livestock, but this does not stop them from being hunted for their meat and hide or being mistaken for a jackal.

Trivia

♦The bat-eared fox derives its name from its large ears that closely resemble those of a bat.

♦Bat-eared foxes eat approximately 1.15 million termites a year

♦The bat-eared fox has more teeth than any other canine.

♦Bat-eared foxes are found in close proximity to plains game such as zebras and antelopes as they feed on the insects that land and feed on their excrement.

♦Bat-eared foxes usually seek out a new den each year before they mate.

♦Bat-eared foxes closely resemble jackals and are sometimes mistaken and killed by locals as a result.

Black-Backed Jackal
(Canis mesomelas)
Swahili: *Bweha nyekundu*

Identification
The black-backed jackal has a long, thin, pointed, fox-like face. Its eyes are large and the ears are large, pointed and upright.

It has a slender body, slender legs and large feet.

Its fur is a gingery, reddish-brown colour. A prominent, well-defined silvery grey saddle of fur runs the length of the jackal's back from the back of the neck to the base of the tail. The chest is white and the throat and underside are a gingery white colour. Scent glands are present on the face and around the anus and genitals.

The long bushy tail is black.

The black-backed jackal has excellent sight, hearing and a keen sense of smell.

The males are larger and more vibrantly coloured than the females.

Body Length	70-90cm
Shoulder Height:	38-50cm
Weight:	5-10kg
Tail Length:	25-35cm

Life Span
Between 8 and 13 years in the wild.

Habitat
Black-backed jackals are adaptable, independent of water and are able to survive in dry, arid countryside. They are usually found in savannahs, grasslands and woodlands.

Behaviour
Black-backed jackals are semi-solitary, either living on their own, as a bonded pair, or as a member of a small family group. Family groups consist of the mother and father, older offspring and the latest litter of cubs. Wary, cunning and adaptable they will either hunt alone, as a mated pair or in a loosely formed pack of five to eight individuals to bring down larger prey (Thomson's gazelles) or scavenge in order to survive. They are able to run at speeds of up to 55km/h, and maintain

a steady running speed of 12-15km/h for longer periods when foraging for food.

They are very territorial, especially a bonded pair who will defend and scent mark the boundaries of their territory with urine and secretions from their scent glands.

The black-backed jackal is diurnal as well as nocturnal.

Diet

The black-backed jackal is an omnivore that feeds on small to medium-sized mammals (rats, mice, mongooses, spring hares), fish, reptiles, birds and insects, as well as fruit, berries and grasses. It is also a scavenger feeding on carrion and on refuse when close to human habitation.

Communication

Black-backed jackals are noisy and will use a variety of vocalisations to communicate with each other—screaming, yelling, growling, whining, woofing, howling and yelping. A loud-pitched howl indicates that prey has been located. When separated from each other they will call out to one another.

Reproduction

Black-backed jackals are monogamous, remaining together for life as a bonded pair, reproducing annually during the dry season (July-October). Both parents are actively involved in rearing the young. The gestation period is between 60-65 days, with the female (vixen) giving birth underground to two to six cubs. New born cubs are blind and helpless. Their eyes, which are initially blue but gradually darken with time, open by the time they are 10 days old. The cubs are hidden in dense thickets or underground burrows for the first few weeks of their life. To avoid the cubs been discovered by predators the females change dens every two weeks, and during this time the male has sole responsibility for defending the territory and hunting. The young are fed regurgitated food until they are two months old and are weaned by the time they are 10-13 weeks old.

By the time the cubs are three months old the den is redundant and they accompany their parents on hunting trips, being able to hunt successfully on their own by the time they are six months old. Between the ages of eight to ten months old they may leave their parents and establish their own territories. Some of the offspring will remain with their parents until they are 18-24 months old before leaving, and others that have left the family group may return to act as helpers, assisting their parents in rearing the latest litter. This affords the cubs some degree of protection from predators and allows the parents to go foraging for food.

Black-backed jackals are sexually mature at eleven months old.

Predators/Threats

They are natural prey for eagles, hyenas, lions and leopards, and may be killed by humans for their fur and meat and if they are a threat to live stock. The majority of the young are killed in the first 14 weeks of life. Loss of habitat is also a threat to their survival.

Trivia

♦The black-backed jackal is also known as the silver-backed jackal or saddle-backed jackal.

♦They have been known to cache food and return 24 hours later to feed on it.

♦They are wary of humans and are not aggressive towards large predators.

♦Black-backed jackals are able to survive in close proximity to human habitation but are more likely to be nocturnal as they will actively scavenge for food among the refuse.

♦Jackals are considered to be vermin by locals as they carry and spread rabies, the canine distemper virus and canine parvovirus.

Genet Cat
Large Spotted Genet Cat (*Genetta tigrina*)
Small Spotted Genet Cat (*Genetta genetta*)
Swahili: *Kanu*

Identification
The two species of genet cat most commonly seen in Kenya and Tanzania are the large spotted genet cat and the small spotted genet cat, and they are very similar to each other.

Large Spotted Genet Cat
The background colour of the large spotted genet cat's fur is yellow-grey. The spots are larger than the small spotted genet cat and are either black or a rusty brown colour. A prominent stripe runs the length of the back and the tail is ringed with a black tip.

Small Spotted Genet Cat
The background colour of the small spotted genet cat's fur is tan to grey. The spots, which are present in rows, are darker than those of the large genet cat. The tail is ringed with a white tip.

Genet cats have a small, fox-like head with large, forward facing, rounded eyes and large, pointed upright ears. Long whiskers are present on the black, pointed snout.

The short, soft fur is varying shades of brown. A combination of spots and a ringed tail provides perfect camouflage.

The body is long with short legs. Five digits are present on each foot and are equipped with sharp retractable claws.

The tail is extremely long and may be up to one and half times the length of its body. This acts as an effective counter balance enabling the genet cat to balance on narrow tree branches and jump from one tree to another.

Genet cats have excellent night vision.

Males are larger than females

Life Span
Eight years in the wild.

Habitat
Genet cats are usually found in riverine woodlands, forests, grasslands and semi-arid deserts. They are also seen in game lodges and can become habituated when in close contact with humans.

Behaviour
A silent, agile, highly skilled hunter, the genet cat is at home hunting prey on the ground as well as in the trees. Their territory is scent marked with urine, claw marks on tree trunks and with a greasy musk-like substance released by the perianal glands. Females are more territorial than males. When threatened the genet cat arches its back and may emit a foul smelling musk-like substance that acts as a deterrent. Their faeces are deposited in clearly marked open latrines.

Genet cats are nocturnal and are particularly active at dusk. They are terrestrial and arboreal.

Diet
Being omnivores they feed on small mammals, birds, bats, reptiles, eggs, frogs, insects, scorpions and fruit. When living close to human habitation, given the opportunity they wilfully kill poultry feeding only on the breast and head.

Communication
A variety of vocalisations are used to communicate their mood, from purring and meowing to spitting.

Reproduction
Genet cats either live in pairs, or if they are solitary they only meet up to mate. The gestation period is 75-90 days. The female can give birth to two litters a year of two to four kittens in a burrow usually between August and March and raises them on her own. The kittens open their eyes and ears after ten days and begin to eat solid food at six weeks. They remain with their mother until they are seven to eight months old and are sexually mature at two years old.

Predators/Threats
Genet cats are natural prey for caracals, serval cats, leopards, owls and pythons. The young are also prey to jackals, civet cats and snakes. They are hunted by locals if they are considered to be a pest.

Trivia

♦Genet cats are able to perform a handstand when releasing a musk-like substance from the specialised perianal glands to scent mark their territory.

♦The musky secretions from the genet cat are used in the pharmaceutical and perfume industries.

♦Ancient Egyptians originally used genet cats to catch rodents, until the introduction of the domestic cat, which did not have the problem of the unpleasant musky secretions.

♦Genet cats can be kept as an exotic pet.

♦The large spotted genet cat is also known as the "blotched genet cat", "rusty spotted genet cat" and "cape genet cat".

♦The small spotted genet cat is known as the "common genet cat".

Leopard Tortoise
(Geochelone pardalis)
Swahili: *Kobe*

Identification

Leopard tortoises are the second largest species of tortoise in Africa and the fourth largest in the world.

The background colour of the hard, lumpy, high-domed shell is pale yellow, and is beautifully marked with an array of black squares that have a brown or yellow inner area with a dark spot in the centre. This central spot reduces in size with age. The markings are unique to each individual and provide the leopard tortoise with perfect camouflage. There is a v-shaped opening at the front of the shell, which allows the head and neck to protrude. When threatened leopard tortoises retract their head and limbs back into the safety of their shells.

The head and limbs are pale yellow.

The leopard tortoise has a hard beak instead of teeth, and this assists in tearing food apart.

The legs are short and are covered by thickened, protective scales. Five claws are present on the paddle-shaped front legs, and four are present on the hind legs. The female's legs are longer than the males and scales are present on the heels of the rear legs to assist with digging.

The tail is short with two to three horny tubercles present and a horny pin.

The tail of the male is longer and thicker than the female's.

Leopard tortoises have very good eyesight, sense of smell and taste. There are no external ear openings; consequently the leopard tortoise has poor hearing.

Males are larger than females.

Length: 45-70cm
Weight: 15–20kg

Habitat

Leopard tortoises are widely distributed throughout sub Saharan Africa and are usually found in semi-arid regions, savannahs and grasslands.

Behaviour

Leopard tortoises are solitary and territorial. They are cold blooded and need to bask in the early morning sun to raise their body temperature. In very hot or cold weather they seek shelter in abandoned animal burrows. They are quite nimble and can move surprisingly quickly over large areas when necessary. They can remain under water for up to ten minutes.

Diet

Leopard tortoises are herbivores with a preference for a high fibre diet. They graze on mixed grasses, wild flowers, beans, thistles, pumpkins, toadstools, watermelons and the pads of the prickly cacti.

Reproduction

Mating is a noisy affair with the male making lots of loud husky calls as well as battering and pushing the female about at the same time. The female digs a hole about 25cm deep in which she lays between 5-30 white eggs at 3 weekly intervals over a period of 20 weeks. The incubation period is between 4-18 months. The hatchlings break the egg shell open with their beaks and then have the arduous task of digging their way to the surface.

Leopard tortoises reach sexual maturity between the ages of 12-15 years old.

Trivia

♦The upper shell is called the *carapace*.

♦In folklore leopard tortoises are associated with strength and immortality.

♦Surprisingly, leopard tortoises are plagued with ticks, mites and internal parasites.

♦The black spots on the leopard tortoise's shell resemble the markings on a leopard—hence the name.

♦Leopard tortoises are reputed to eat old bones.

Rock Hyrax
(*Procavia capensis*)
Bush Hyrax
(*Heterohyrax brucei*)
Swahili: *Pimbi*

Identification

Hyraxes are small rodent-like mammals found throughout most of Africa.

They have a round head, with small rounded ears, large dark eyes and a black truncated nose. Long whiskers are present on their muzzles. They use their molars in preference to their tusk-like incisors to bite food. The incisors are used primarily in defence.

The hyrax has a small, rotund, muscular body with short, stubby legs. The feet have smooth, rubbery pads that are moist due to the presence of sweat glands enabling the hyrax to climb difficult rocky surfaces, but are not suitable for digging or burrowing. Four toes are present on the foreleg and three toes on the hind leg. Small hoof-like nails are present on the tip of each toe, apart from the inner toe of the hind foot, which has a claw used for grooming and scratching.

The fur is short and coarse. The bush hyrax is light grey to brown in colour whereas the rock hyrax is light to dark brown. The underside is creamy white. The presence of long tactile hairs over their bodies enables the hyrax to orientate itself in dark, enclosed places. A distinct circular sweat gland on the back is covered by a patch of long hair that may be a black or yellow colour, and becomes erect when the hyrax is excited.

The tail is little more than a stump and is not visible.

The male hyrax is slightly bigger than the female.

Physiology

The hyrax has difficulty regulating and maintaining its bodily temperature. It relies on basking in the sun and huddling together to generate warmth, and retreating to its shelter to cool down if it overheats.

Life Span

Between 8-10 years in the wild. Females usually live longer than males.

Habitat

Hyraxes are terrestrial and are usually found in savannahs, mountains or forests, and can survive at altitudes as low as 400m below sea level right up to 3,800m above sea level. They are unable to dig, so live in shelters that are naturally occurring crevices in kopjes, cliffs and boulders. They are tolerant of arid conditions.

Behaviour

Hyraxes live in colonies of up to 50 individuals. The colonies are made up of several small, stable family groups. The group consists of:

A single, dominant, territorial male who may control more than one group.

Three to seven females. Females are not territorial.

Subordinate males who fall into one of three sub groups.

Peripheral males that are tolerated, but live on the periphery of the dominant males territory, and who in the absence of the dominant male will attempt to take over the group.

Early dispersing males who leave the group when they are 16-24 months old.

Late dispersing males who leave the group before they are 30 months old.

Hyraxes are shy but are particularly vicious when threatened. They are found in close proximity to their shelters, either huddling together to keep warm, basking in the sun or feeding. Feeding is a group activity with members facing outwards, looking out for predators. There is also a male or female on sentry duty who will raise the alarm when threatened.

Hyraxes urinate and defecate in the same spot, and their latrines are easily identified by the white deposits of un-dissolved calcium carbonate from the urine that covers the rocks.

Hyraxes are diurnal.

Diet

Hyraxes are herbivores and are able to feed on vegetation of poor nutritional value. They feed on grasses, vegetables, herbs, bark, stems, buds, leaves and fruit. Their kidneys are efficient and enable them to exist on the minimum amount of water.

Communication

Hyraxes use a wide range of vocalisations to communicate with each other from growling, shrieking, squealing, whistling and raucous alarm calls to twittering.

Reproduction

Hyraxes live in a polygamous harem. During the mating season, solitary males will attempt to mate with any available female. Consequently, dominant males are particularly aggressive towards any other males.

The females give birth to between one to four young during the rainy season after a gestation period of 212-245 days

The young are born fully developed, covered in fur and with their eyes open, and are able to run and jump about within one hour of being born. They begin to eat vegetation when they are two days old and are weaned between one and five months old. The young play together in a nursery group.

Hyraxes are sexually mature by the time they are 16-18 months old. Males leave the maternal group between 16-30 months. Females remain with the maternal group

Predators/Threats

Hyraxes are natural prey for African wild dogs, caracals, serval cats, civet cats, jackals, leopards, lions, mongooses, snakes (pythons in particular) and large birds. They are hunted by humans for their meat and skin. Loss of habitat is also a threat to their survival.

Trivia

♦Hyraxes are related to elephants, having similar teeth, leg and foot bones.

♦The hyraxes' incisors continue to grow throughout life.

♦The bush hyrax is also known as the yellow spotted hyrax.

♦Hyraxes produce vast quantities of dung and urine that is used in traditional medicine to treat epilepsy and convulsions. The burnt hair of the hyrax is mixed with ash and water to make a drink that treats coughs.

♦Hyraxes are nicknamed "rock rabbits", "dassies", "conies", "shrewmice" and "rock badgers".

♦Hyraxes can become tame when living close to human habitation.

Warthog
(Phacochoerus aethiopicus)
Swahili: *Ngiki/Ngiri/Gwasi*

Identification

The warthog has a large head with a short, thickened neck. It has a muscular, stocky body, long legs with tiny, hoofed feet and is capable of running at speeds of 55km/h.

The warthog's large, flat head is out of proportion with its body (one sixth of the total head and body length). The eyes are small and are set high on the head to compensate for its poor eyesight.

The nostrils are located on the end of a long, rounded, rubbery snout and point downwards. This assists the warthog when rooting for food that is underground.

Two pairs of short, sharp tusks protrude from either side of the snout. The upper tusks are long and curve upwards. The tusks are used in self defence and for rooting and digging up food. They have 32-34 long and sharp canine teeth.

Depending on the sex, two or three pairs of facial warts are present. The male has three pairs of warts, one pair beneath the eyes, (these protect the eyes when the warthog engages in fighting), a pair on the snout near the tusks, and a pair on the lower jaw. The female has two pairs of warts (they are absent on the snout). The warts are formed from thickened growths of cartilage that become more prominent with age.

The ears are large and mobile.

The warthog's wrinkled skin is a brownish black colour. There is a sparse covering of hair over the whole body. A long, coarse mane of dark brown hair extends from the top of the head as far as the middle of the back.

There is a tuft of hair on the tip of the long, thin tail.

The warthog has a good sense of smell and an acute sense of hearing.

Body Length: 90cm-1.5m
Shoulder Height: 63-85cm
Tail Length: 25-50cm
Weight: Male 60-100kg
Female 45-70kg

Upper Tusk:	Male	23-60cm
	Female	15-25cm
Lower Tusk:	15cm	

Life Span
Fifteen years in the wild.

Habitat
Warthogs are usually found in savannahs, grasslands, and woodlands, in or near waterholes. They can be found up to altitudes of 2,000m.

Behaviour
Warthogs usually live in a small, matriarchal group called a sounder, which consists of one to two females (sows), their young (piglets) and yearlings. The sounder can sometimes contain as many as 40 warthogs. Adult males (boars) only associate with the females during the mating season. Male warthogs are not territorial and either live in a bachelor group or have a solitary existence.

Warthogs spend the daylight hours foraging for food, particularly in the early morning and evening. They feed by resting on their forelegs and use their snouts to uproot food. They like to lie close to each other in the shade and to wallow in mud.

They sleep and shelter in abandoned burrows at night time. The young enter the burrow first, followed by the adults who go in backwards. This enables them to defend the burrow from intruders, as well as making a swift exit if predators appear close by. Warthogs are extremely fast and agile, and are difficult for a predator to catch.

Warthogs are diurnal.

Diet
The warthog is essentially a grazer, but is also considered to be omnivorous. It feeds primarily on roots, grass, herbs, bark, fruit and berries but will also eat insects, scorpions, earthworms, small mammals, birds, reptiles and carrion. Warthogs eat soil, bones and other animal dung to compensate for any trace minerals and elements that may be absent from their diet.

Communication

Warthogs are usually quiet but can use a range of vocalisations to communicate with each other—grunting, growling snorting and squealing. When alarmed or threatened they will retreat to their underground shelter. Warthogs also communicate by scent marking.

Reproduction

Mating takes place in May and June. Males are only found in the presence of females when mating. During the mating season they regularly engage in fights with other males to establish mating rights. The facial warts protect them from serious injury.

The gestation period is up to 175 days. The female withdraws from the sounder to give birth to two to four piglets in a grass lined burrow. This occurs during the dry season in October and November. The piglets emerge from the burrow at two weeks old and are completely weaned at three to four months old. When the female gives birth, any remaining piglets from previous litters are driven away, but they may rejoin the group at a later date. Male warthogs leave their mothers at 15 months old, but females may remain with the sounder for life.

Warthogs reach sexual maturity between 18-24 months old.

Predators/Threats

Warthogs are common. They are natural prey for lions, cheetahs, leopards, jackal, crocodiles, African wild dogs and hyenas. Eagles and jackals are the main threat to the young.

Warthogs are symptomless carriers of African swine fever, and if there is an outbreak, locals will actively hunt and kill them. The same applies if they raid their crops in search of food.

Trivia

♦Warthogs are the only swine to defecate together, 4-14 times a day.

♦Warthogs run with their tails up in the air.

♦The warthog's lack of fur and fat means they are vulnerable to the rays of the sun and low temperatures. Shelter is therefore very important and necessary for them.

♦Warthogs support the blood-sucking tsetse fly, which carries sleeping sickness.

Translocation

Translocation is the planned or emergency relocation of an individual or group of wild animals from one area to another, and may be for one of the following reasons:

In areas that are densely populated, the animals are in direct competition with each other on a daily basis for food and water.

It is usual to move the animals to areas that are under populated and have abundant supplies of food. Without human intervention the animals could face hunger, starvation and ultimately death.

The plains grazers can adversely affect plant life in one of two ways:

actual damage to the plant itself, such as removal of bark from trees, uprooting of plants or partial damage which prevents a plant from thriving.

a continued high concentration of animals feeding on the same vegetation can put some plants at risk of extinction.

Out on the open plains, there exists a common and mutual interdependency between the plains grazers. The heavy grazers (elephants, hippos, buffaloes) trample and feed on tall coarse grasses, making way for the intermediate grazers (zebras, wildebeest, hartebeest) who feed on shorter grasses. The remaining short grass and shoots are eaten by the smallest and lightest herbivores (dik dik, warthogs, Thompson's gazelle). This delicately balanced relationship can be disrupted by the absence of the heavy or intermediate grazers. The translocation of animals to an area of dense overgrowth can clear the way for the lighter grazers.

Animals in national parks and game reserves can come into conflict with the local population, and this has to be managed sensitively. The

parks and reserves need to maintain a good relationship, and the good will of the local community. Elephants in particular, in their search for food and water, can break down boundary fences and escape into the surrounding countryside. They destroy the local inhabitants' property, raid their crops and deprive them of their livelihood. They either have to be translocated or have a radio collar fitted. The collar enables rangers to track their movements, so that they can be moved on if they get too close to human habitation.

Translocation returns or reintroduces an animal back to its natural environment.

The translocation of animals encourages the development of the tourist "safari industry" in developing, underdeveloped and deprived areas. This provides employment for the local population, and vital funds to sustain and maintain the parks and reserves.

Animals may be translocated to increase the number of breeding stock and ensure survival of the species.

Animals can be translocated if their survival is being threatened by poachers.

The only other alternative to translocation is to cull the animals.

Translocation of animals is a difficult and dangerous job and requires a coordinated, experienced, highly skilled team of experts. The team is made up of pilots, marksmen, vets, winch operators, drivers, groundskeepers and rangers.

A helicopter or light aircraft may be used to identify and locate suitable animals for relocation. The helicopter herds the animal to a suitable area for darting and recovery. The animals may be darted from the air or by a marksman on the ground.

After an individual animal has succumbed to the tranquilliser, it is medically checked, blindfolded, ropes are applied and as it regains consciousness it is manoeuvred into a crate onto an awaiting truck.

When a group of animals needs to be translocated they are rounded up by a helicopter and driven into a boma. A boma is a massive trap with canvass side curtains that act as a funnel. The animals are driven down the funnel and onto the awaiting truck.

On arrival at their destination the animals are "free released" safely back into the wild.

Diseases affecting wildlife

African Swine Fever

African Swine Fever (ASF) is a serious, highly contagious viral disease that spreads rapidly and affects domestic pigs. Although African wild pigs (warthogs, bush pigs, giant forest pigs) are the natural carriers of the swine fever virus, they do not actually go on to develop swine fever. Soft-bodied ticks are also carriers of the virus.

Swine fever is transmitted by direct contact between infected animals whether dead or alive, via bodily secretions, excretions, semen and blood that may be inseminated, ingested or come into contact with mucous membranes or an open wound. The incubation period is between 5-15 days. The onset of the disease is rapid once signs and symptoms appear, with death occurring within 1-7 days. The animal presents with fever, discharges from the eyes and nose, loss of appetite, vomiting, diarrhoea, lethargy and blue/red blotching of the skin of the extremities.

Swine fever is endemic in warthogs and leads to locals killing them in order to protect domestic livestock.

Anthrax

Anthrax is one of the world's oldest and deadliest diseases. An invisible and silent killer, its spores can lie dormant for decades until conditions are right for it to wreak havoc on the animal world.

Anthrax does not necessarily pass from animal to animal, the spores are either inhaled, ingested or enter the body through an open wound or a bite. The spores live in dry soil, and dry weather conditions are perfect, as the animals have to dig and root deeper for food. The spores are disturbed and ingested, and once inside the animal's body they multiply rapidly. Deadly toxins decimate the immune system and cause fatal haemorrhaging resulting in death.

A dead carcass is often a source of infection as it quickly attracts predators, scavengers and blow flies to the scene. Vultures are resistant to anthrax and infected meat passes straight through their acidic digestive system. When feeding on the carcass however, their head, neck and body are covered in the anthrax spores that can be unwittingly passed on to other animals.

Anthrax is often seen as being nature's way of culling wild animals.

Bovine Tuberculosis

Bovine tuberculosis (TB) is one of the most widespread infectious diseases in the world, affecting large numbers of domestic livestock (cattle, pigs, horses, dogs), wildlife (buffalo, wildebeest, topi, kudu) and humans alike.

Tuberculosis is caused by the bacteria *Mycobacterium bovis* and is transmitted between domestic livestock, wildlife and humans by inhalation (coughing, sneezing) ingestion (eating infected meat or carcasses) and through open wounds.

This is a progressive, debilitating disease that is hard to detect and primarily affects the respiratory system. Depending on the state of the immune system TB can take years to develop, the disease progresses slowly by initially damaging the lungs, affecting the lymph glands and then spreading to other organs. This is accompanied by weight loss and reduced exercise tolerance, which weakens the animal and results in death.

Out in the wild predators and scavengers can spread the disease to each other by inhaling nasal droplets and oral secretions, eating carcasses and drinking water from the same source.

Foot-and-Mouth Disease

Swahili: *Ugonjwa wa midomo na miguu*

Foot-and-mouth disease (FMD) is a highly contagious, fatal, viral infection that affects cloven-hoofed animals throughout the world.

Foot and mouth disease is caused by the FMD virus *Aphthovirus* and is capable of spreading rapidly over long distances, affecting domestic livestock and wild animals alike.

The virus is transmitted by animals that have close contact with each other, either directly or indirectly by inhalation, ingestion or through open wounds and mucous membranes. The virus is present in all infected animals' secretions (saliva, expired air) and excretions (urine, faeces) as well as in milk and semen. It may also be present in standing water and in waste food. Humans who have close contact with animals can spread the disease as the virus may be present on their clothing or body.

The animals are infected within hours of exposure to the virus. The incubation period is between 2-14 days. The animal presents with high fever, excessive salivation and blistering of the lips, tongue and feet.

It is a painful disease; the animals have difficulty eating and walking. This is accompanied by weight loss, lameness and possible secondary infection from the blisters. The animals recover eventually, but may develop myocarditis in the interim period and die.

Foot-and-mouth disease affects domestic livestock (cattle, sheep, goats, pigs) and wildlife (buffalo, giraffes, zebras, warthogs, camels, wildebeest, kudu).

Wildlife are usually infected by contact with domestic livestock.

Rabies

Swahili: *Kichaa cha mwba*

Rabies, or *hydrophobia*, is one of the most feared viral diseases in the world, affecting all warm-blooded animals (including humans), and is prevalent in the continents of Asia, Africa, America and Europe.

Rabies is contagious and caused by the *Lyssa* virus. It is a disease that can pass freely between animals and humans.

The rabies virus is present in saliva and is transmitted via an animal bite that breaks the skin and enters the blood stream. It can, on rare occasions, be transmitted by an animal licking an open wound or having contact with the mucous membranes of the eyes, nose, mouth and throat. Once infected the animal can carry the virus for a period of ten days to six months before showing any symptoms of the disease, although sometimes the virus can be carried for several years.

The virus grows undetected by the immune system in the cells of muscle tissue. The virus then travels along the nerve pathways towards the brain. The nearer to the brain that the bite takes place, the faster the development of the disease. Once the brain is inflamed (encephalitis) symptoms appear quickly and the disease progresses rapidly, there is no cure or treatment at this point and only one outcome—death. The rabies virus is only present in saliva once the disease has affected the brain. Up to that point a bite from a rabid animal does not carry the risk of infection.

Rabies is difficult to diagnose in wild animals as there are no typical signs and symptoms. There are two forms of rabies in animals.

The **furious form** where the animal is initially agitated and aggressive, biting at anything and foaming at the mouth. Shortly before death, the animal becomes paralysed.

The other form is **dumb rabies**. The animal is lethargic and depressed. Once again paralysis occurs shortly before death.

Rinderpest

Swahili: *Sotoka*

Rinderpest (RP) is a highly contagious viral disease with a high mortality rate that affects cloven-hoofed ungulates such as domestic livestock (cattle, sheep, goats, pigs) and some species of wildlife (giraffes). It is particularly common in Africa, the Indian subcontinent and the Middle East.

Rinderpest is caused by the *Morbilliviru* virus. Inhalation of expired air is believed to be the primary source of exposure to the virus, followed closely by contact with nasal secretions, eye discharges and saliva, or urine and faeces of the infected animal. Rinderpest may also be transmitted by ingesting contaminated food and water.

Rinderpest is characterised by its sudden presentation. The incubation period is short, between two to nine days, after which the animal shows symptoms of high fever, inflamed mucous membranes, nasal discharges, gastroenteritis, constipation and later profuse diarrhoea. Death follows swiftly.

The spread of the disease is facilitated by the movement of infected animals in the following ways:

♦The frequent movement of animals by herdsmen in search of new pastures for cattle to graze on.

♦Sales of animals at markets.

♦Illegal movement of livestock across borders.

♦Cattle rustling.

♦Seasonal movement of wildlife in search of food and water bringing them into contact with domestic livestock.

♦Domestic livestock can wander into national parks and reserves and transmit the disease to wildlife.

♦In the wild buffalo, eland, giraffes, kudu, wild pigs and warthogs are highly susceptible to rinderpest. Antelope and hippopotamuses are less susceptible.

♦Rinderpest does not affect humans.

Habitats-Savannah

Savannahs or savannas are tropical grasslands found between 5° and 15° north and south of the equator where the average temperature is 28°C and the annual rainfall is between 75-125cm. They are found in Africa, Madagascar, northern South America, India, Australia and Myanmar and Thailand in South East Asia. They are a transitional  zone between tropical rain forests and deserts. Savannahs are where the majority of wildlife covered in this book are found, and they are often referred to as the African Plains, with the largest and most well-known being the Serengeti.

Climate
Savannahs are warm to hot all year round (20-35°C) and are characterised by two clearly defined seasons:

The dry season (winter), which is a prolonged period of drought.

The wet/rainy season (summer), which is a concentrated period of heavy rainfall. The amount of rain that falls varies from one year to the next.

Soil
The soil of the savannah is called laterite and is porous, acidic and of poor nutritional value. The soil is soaked in the wet season and is baked dry in the dry season, as a result a hardened crust forms which is difficult for plant roots to penetrate. The soil is fragile and is easily broken down and fragmented by the pressure of animals' hooves. Heavy grazing by domestic livestock and cultivation of crops reduces groundcover and depletes the soil of it nutrients.

Termite mounds can be seen on the savannah and are important in soil formation as well as providing food and shelter for animals.

Vegetation
Savannahs are large, rolling, open, semi-arid landscapes, whose plant life has evolved to cope with alternating prolonged periods of drought and seasonal rainfall.

Annual rainfall dictates the type of vegetation that is able to survive in this environment. The plants are all in competition with each other for water.

Between 10-20cm of rain per annum only allows grasses to grow. Up to 30cm of rain per annum allows shrubs to grow.

Over 30cm of rain per annum allows the occasional tree to grow, such as the acacia tree, which is synonymous with the African savannah.

Above 40cm of rain per annum encourages and supports the growth of trees that are now able to form a canopy, putting the grasses in the shade and restricting their growth.

The open canopy of the savannah encourages the growth of perennial grasses that dominant the landscape. The grasses turn yellow and die back during the dry season but burst back to life at the first sign of rain. Seeds can lie dormant for long periods until conditions are favourable, allowing them to burst into life. The grasses grow vigorously and can be as high as 1.8m.

The trees of the savannah have evolved to survive prolonged periods of drought. Long, deep tap roots enable them to dig deep into the earth to seek out water, and the large trunks are able to store water. Fewer leaves reduces water loss, as do small waxy leaves. Deciduous trees lose their leaves in the dry season to conserve water. Thickened bark, which is either corky or of a smooth resinous consistency, is fire resistant. Some trees like the acacia tree are browser resistant, producing phenols that make the leaves unpalatable and cause the browsing animal to move on. They also produce ethylene, which stimulates surrounding trees to produce phenols.

The bushes have sharp thorns that reduce water loss and deter the browsers.

Fires

The growth of vegetation on the savannah is kept in check by periodic bush fires, which may be natural (electrical storms), or in some cases caused by humankind.

Poachers may set fire to the savannah as a means of exposing and moving the animals. It is not unusual to see a marabou stork standing patiently in front of a wall of fire waiting to capture the escaping wildlife. After a fire all that remains is a fine covering of blackened, powdery ash that makes the soil fertile. The deep, starch roots of the grasses remain unharmed during a fire. When the rains return, the grasses sprout again, and life is restored to the savannah.

Animals

No other environment on earth is able to equal the savannah's ability to support the large numbers and wide variety of mammals that co-exist here. Large herds of browsing and grazing plains game (herbivores), live here under the watchful eye of the ever present predators—the carnivores and scavengers.

Herbivores consume large amounts of food and influence the growth of vegetation on the savannah. The majority of the animals are grazers (wildebeest, zebra, Cape buffalo), some are browsers (giraffes) and some are a combination of both (elephant, impala, duiker, gerenuk). Continued grazing keeps the growth of the grasses in check and promotes the growth of weeds. The individual grazers are highly selective and have a preference for the height and type of grass they will eat. The heavy grazers (elephants, hippopotamuses, roan antelope, sable antelope, buffaloes), have a preference for long, tall, coarse grass, exposing the medium-sized grasses for the intermediate grazers (zebras). The smaller, selective herbivores (gazelles, warthogs) follow in the tracks of the intermediate herbivores, feeding on the remaining short grasses, shoots and roots. This is known as the grazing succession. The animals excrete sodium and nitrogen, which is necessary for plant growth.

The dry season causes the animals to migrate in search of food and water. It is usual at this time to find a high concentration of animals near the water-holes, the grazers and browsers drinking water and the predators waiting to ambush them. As the grasses dry out on the savannah they provide perfect camouflage for some of the predators.

Wooded areas support a reduced number of browsers compared with the grasslands. As a result the browsers are usually solitary or live in small herds. The browsers control the growth and proliferation of woody vegetation, with some trees and shrubs never reaching their full size. Elephants are particularly destructive as they eat leaves and twigs, break branches, strip the bark from the trunk and are ultimately capable of uprooting a tree. In some areas they may be culled because of the damage they cause to the plant life, whereas in other areas they may be translocated.

The scavengers (hyenas, jackals, vultures) always get a poor press but actually play a vital role in cleaning up the savannah, ridding it of diseased, sick animals and their remains. Any remaining animal horns or bones provide vital food for the larvae of moths. Dung beetles deal with animal faeces.

♦Savannahs cover 25% of the land on Earth.

♦The savannahs cover 40% of the land in Africa, which equates to about 5 million sq mi.

♦In the savannahs of East Africa the majority of the plains game give birth to their young at the start of the wet season when there is an abundance of food. If the rains fail, this can seriously affect the survival of the newly born calves.

♦The word *savannah* comes from a 14th-century word that means "land which is without trees but with much grass either short or tall". By the late 19th century its meaning changed to "land with both grass and trees".

Habitats-Miombo Woodlands

Miombo woodlands are mature, deciduous, tropical woodlands and dry forests found in central, western and southern Tanzania where the average temperature is between 15 and 30°C. The miombo woodlands in central Tanzania are classified as "dry" as they receive less than 100cm of rain per annum, whereas the miombo woodlands in south-west Tanzania are classified as "wet" as they receive more than 100cm of rain per annum. Broad, interspersed grazing depressions are a feature of the miombo woodlands.

The trees have adapted to withstand prolonged periods of drought, variable seasonal rainfall, and well drained soil that is acidic and of poor nutritional value. They lose their leaves in the dry season to conserve moisture, producing new leaves before the wet season starts. Their fruit is used to provide food for livestock, and the wood can be used for crafts, construction or as fuel.

Fires are frequent in miombo woodlands during the dry season. These fires may be natural (electrical storms), or in some cases caused by humankind. Locals seeking fresh pastures for cultivation or grazing will set fire to the woodlands.

Miombo woodlands provide the ideal habitat for a large, diverse number of African animals — African wild dogs, antelopes, black rhinoceroses, Cape buffaloes, caracals, cheetahs, colobus monkeys, duikers, elands, elephants, giraffes, hartebeests, hippopotamuses, hyenas, jackals, kudus, lions, leopards, mongooses, Nile crocodiles, oribis, reedbucks, rhinoceroses, sable antelopes, warthogs, waterbucks and zebras.

Trivia
♦Miombo woodlands cover one third of the land in Tanzania.

♦Miombo woodlands are being deforested at an alarming rate, and are not sustainable.

♦The presence of the tsetse fly, which carries sleeping sickness, deters humans from settling in these areas.

♦Miombo woodlands are only found in Mikumi National Park, Ruaha National Park and Selous Game Reserve.

Habitats - Semi-Arid Deserts
Semi-arid deserts are inhospitable, rough, rugged environments. The ground is covered with either fine sand or loose, lava-like rocky gravel. Only thorn scrub, hardy grasses, weeds and hardy nomads live here. They have clearly defined seasons:

Long, warm, dry summers with drought-like conditions, and temperatures falling to 10°C during the night.

A short winter season with erratic, heavy showers where less than 70cm of rain falls per annum.

Semi-arid deserts are found in northern Kenya and parts of north-eastern and central Tanzania.

Habitats-Termites
Swahili: *Mchwa*

Termites are tiny, soft bodied insects (less than 2mm). They are herbivorous, feeding on dry grass, plant roots, wood, bark, straw and any other plant matter that comes their way. Bacteria produced in the stomach digests the cellulose. The termite's high fat and protein content makes it a valuable source of food for animals such as the aardvark and humans.

The colony, in which up to 5 million termites live, has a highly organised social structure or caste system made up of:

◆A king.

◆A primary queen. This is the first termite to find and establish the colony, she may be over 12cm long and can lay up to 30,000 eggs a day, for 15 years.

◆Secondary queens who take over if the primary queen dies or is killed.

◆Soldiers, who defend and protect the termite mound/nest from intruders, such as ants.

◆Workers, who gather and store food, build and repair the nest and look after the eggs and larvae. They are blind and wingless and die quickly from exposure to the sun if they are outside the nest for any length of time.

◆Reproductives, who have wings and fly round in swarms trying to set up new nests.

Termites produce a chemical called a pheromone, which is used to establish social order and map out trails to and from the nest.

Termites live and operate underground, building large, elaborate and monumental termite mounds from saliva and particles of soil. The mounds, which are found in the tropics and dry savannahs, are in areas of good drainage and can be up to 6m high and 30m in diameter. Termites can dig to depths of 75m in search of water, bringing everything from below to the surface. This activity aerates the soil and adds nutrients to it. The mound gets higher and higher the more they dig. An active colony is constantly adding to, and repairing, the mound.

The temperature (28°C-30°C) and humidity inside the mound is constant and is maintained by a series of air ducts. Hot air rises and leaves via the air ducts and outside winds send air currents down into the underground chambers.

The mound is made up of series of chambers with interconnecting tunnels. Faeces and saliva are used to construct the partitioning walls. Inside there are segregated areas for breeding, egg development and gardening.

The mound is usually vacated when the queen dies or is killed, and is either inhabited by a new colony of termites or becomes home to warthogs, squirrels, hyenas, dwarf mongoose, black mambas or porcupines. Termite mounds make useful look out points for leopards and cheetahs.

Trivia

♦Termites are sometimes referred to as white ants, although they are not related to ants.

♦Termites have been known to feed on dung.

♦Termites can devastate crops of maize and millet.

♦Ants may attack the termites and invade their nest.

Habitats-Kopje

A *kopje* is a rocky outcrop or island that rises abruptly from the African plains. They are made of ancient granite rock and are covered in shrubs, grasses and wild sisal. They offer shade, shelter and sanctuary to wildlife in the wild, hostile and inhospitable environment of the African plains, and are often frequented by cheetahs, dik-diks, rock hyraxes, bush hyraxes, mongooses and snakes.

Vegetation

Acacia Tree
Swahili: *Mgunga*

The acacia tree or umbrella tree is synonymous with the African savannah. A slow-growing, drought-resistant tree, it grows to a height of 20m and thrives in the arid conditions of the savannah, grasslands and sand dunes of Africa. It has a deep, widespread tap root that enables it to survive the dry season, and a flattened canopy that spans 8-13m and provides welcome shelter to animals in the heat of the midday sun. The black-grey bark is rough, the leaves are small to minimise water loss and it has thorns that grow in pairs on the branches. Pale, clustered, aromatic flowers growing on old wood cover the acacia tree in early summer. Protein and carbohydrate-rich seed pods are produced by the acacia tree and are a welcome source of food to animals (kudu, impala, rhino, elephant) in the dry season.

Defence Mechanism
When a giraffe begins browsing on an acacia tree, the tree increases the levels of phenols in its remaining leaves making them unpalatable. As the giraffe continues browsing on the tree, the leaves become more and more unpalatable and this prompts the giraffe to move on. At the same time, ethylene is emitted by the acacia tree, which stimulates other trees in the surrounding area (as far as 50m away) to increase their production of phenols. Consequently giraffes only feed on one acacia tree in ten.

Trivia

♦The acacia tree is mentioned in the Bible in the Book of Exodus and Book of Isaiah and is referred to as *Shitta*.

♦The biblical Ark of the Covenant was constructed from the acacia tree.

Baobab Tree
(Adansonia digitata)
Swahili: *Mbuyu tree*

The baobab tree is an ancient, slow-growing deciduous tree found at low altitudes in the hot, dry and arid regions of Africa, India and Australia.

The baobab has an enormous cylindrical trunk, which is between 7-15m in diameter. During the rainy season the girth of the baobab tree increases to accommodate the 120,000 litres of water that it is capable of storing, shrinking back to its original size during the dry season. The fire-resistant, cork-like bark is 5-10cm thick and is a grey-brown colour. Damaged bark is quickly replaced by new bark allowing the tree to continue to grow and thrive.

The baobab is leafless for up to nine months of the year, during which time its thick, tapering, root-like branches are left exposed giving it the appearance of having been planted upside down, hence the nickname upside-down tree.

The leaves are divided into five to seven leaflets on a single stalk.

Large, pendulous, sweetly scented white flowers, between 17-20cm in diameter, open late afternoon from October to December. The flowers are pollinated by bats and bush babies during the night and die within 24 hours of opening. The dying flowers turn brown and fall to the ground, acquiring an unpleasant odour as they decay.

The fruit of the baobab is egg shaped. The outer woody shell is either a dark green or brown colour and is covered in tiny yellow-brown hairs. The white, powdery pulp inside the fruit surrounds black, kidney-shaped seeds.

A mature baobab can grow as high as 25-30m.

Uses of the Baobab Tree

Local inhabitants refer to the baobab as the "tree of life" as it provides food, water, shade and shelter to humans and animals alike.

Mature baobab trunks are hollow inside and have been

used as pubs, storage barns, houses and prisons. Birds, small rodents, squirrels, bush babies, lizards, snakes, scorpions and insects all make their home in various parts of the tree.

The bark is used to make paper, cloth, nets, mats, baskets, snares, string and rope, and the roots are used to make cosmetics and tonics. The leaves are used as a vegetable and are a rich source of vitamin C, calcium, sugars and potassium. They may be eaten fresh, dried or boiled to make a spinach-like soup. The flowers provide nectar for fruit bats and bush babies and the pollen is used to make glue.

The fruit is a rich source of vitamin C and tartaric acid and is used to make a refreshing drink that tastes like lemonade. The pith can be chewed to provide moisture or may be used medicinally to treat fevers. Wild animals such as baboons, monkeys, antelopes and elephants all eat the fallen fruit.

The seeds are either used to aid the fermentation of beer, as a thickener for soups or roasted to make a coffee-like beverage. An oil-like substance can be extracted from the seeds, which can be used as fuel or as a dye.

Trivia

◆The baobab has numerous nicknames:

Dead rat tree. The fruit pods resemble rats hanging upside down by their tails.

Cream of tartar tree
Monkey-bread tree
Lemonade tree

◆The baobab only produces flowers after it is 20 years old.

◆Baobab trees can be 1,000 years old. Some are reported to be between 2,000-3,000 years old. Unlike other trees the baobab does not produce growth rings by which the age of the tree can be estimated. ◆Radiocarbon dating is used to accurately calculate the age of the baobab.

◆Superstitious locals believe that picking the flowers of the baobab brings them bad luck, and could mean that they may be eaten by a lion. On the brighter side, soaking the seeds in water and drinking it is believed to prevent attacks from crocodiles.

♦When the baobab dies, it rots from the inside outwards, eventually collapsing in a heap leaving only a mass of fibres behind.

♦Baobab oil is extracted from the seeds and is high in Vitamins A, D, E and F and has been a part of African skincare for centuries. The oil is said to have impressive moisturising properties.

Euphorbia Tree

Euphorbia trees are found in temperate regions of the world, as well as subtropical and tropical regions of the Americas and Africa. This succulent species originates from Africa and the Americas. They grow at low altitudes, in deciduous woodlands with well drained soil and are tolerant of drought conditions.

The euphorbia tree is tall, upright, with multiple branches and has a cactus-like appearance. The main stem and branches are thick and fleshy and are coloured dark green with pale green and white stripes. The short-lived leaves are small. It flowers in April and produces fruit in August that is eaten by birds

The euphorbia tree produces a milky white sap called latex, which is poisonous and extremely caustic, blistering the skin and mouth and burning the delicate mucous membranes of the eyes, nose and mouth. In severe cases it can cause blindness.

Trivia

♦The euphorbia tree is known as the "milk bush", the "cathedral cactus" and the "candelabra tree".

♦The sap of the euphorbia trees has been used as a purgative.

♦Black rhinos are able to feed on the euphorbia tree with no ill effect.

♦Locals catch fish by using the sap of the euphorbia tree in ponds to paralyse them, after which they rise to the surface. They also use the sap to kill maggots in the open wounds of domestic livestock.

Sausage Tree
(Kigelia pinnata or Kigelia africana)
Swahili: Mburu

The sausage tree is a semi-deciduous tree that grows in the tropical regions of Africa, usually close to rivers and streams.

The sausage tree grows upright for several years before developing branches that form a wide spreading canopy. The trunk is short and thick, and the grey bark shows signs of peeling with age. Underlying wood is a pale yellowy brown colour.

Lime green, leathery leaflets grow on a long stalk with a single leaf at the tip. In areas where there is rain throughout the year the sausage tree is evergreen, but in areas where there is a long dry season or prolonged drought it will shed its leaves to conserve moisture.

Fragrantly scented, orangey-purple-red bell-shaped flowers grow in small clusters on long stems between July and October. The flowers open early evening and are pollinated by bats and insects.

Distinct, sausage-like fruit hang from rope-like stalks and fall to the ground from May onwards. A thin, grey skin covers the fibrous inner pulp that surrounds the wingless seeds. The fruit can be 30-60cm long and weigh between 5-10kg.

Sausage trees grow as high as 20m.

Uses of the Sausage Tree

♦The wood of the sausage tree is used to make oars and yokes.

♦The leaves are eaten by elephants and kudus and are used by locals to feed livestock.

♦Fallen flowers are eaten by wild animals—impala, kudu and nyala.

♦Unripe fruit is inedible and poisonous.

♦The fruit is eaten by bush pigs, porcupines, elephants, giraffes, hippopotamuses, baboons and monkeys. It is used in shampoos and skin preparations and medicinally to treat warts, cuts, sores, rheumatism, syphilis and snake bites.

♦Baked fruit is an aid to fermenting beer. Boiled fruit produces a red dye.

♦Locals roast and eat the seeds as famine food.

Trivia

♦The sausage tree is nicknamed "the fat tail of the sheep".

♦Falling fruit can cause serious injury to people and substantial damage to vehicles.

♦The sausage tree is tolerant of drought conditions but susceptible to frost.

♦Fresh, unripe fruit is poisonous and has a purgative affect on the bowels.

Travel Care

Before you go

Contact your GP practice six to eight weeks before you go on holiday. This will give the doctor, practice nurse and pharmacists enough time to order, organise and arrange the necessary vaccinations and medication. To save time, find out from the practice reception staff if you need to complete a questionnaire before seeing the doctor/nurse. The questionnaire usually asks for information about your planned trip—destination, duration of trip, activities and types of accommodation. The doctor/practice nurse will then decide whether or not they need to see you.

Travel advice, vaccinations and medication are not part of the core NHS Services, therefore the GP practice may charge you.

Some of the vaccinations are not routinely available on the NHS and will require payment. Some medications require a private prescription and payment. When processing a private prescription it is worth shopping around local pharmacists and supermarkets as many are prepared to give discounts.

Vaccinations required for visits to Kenya & Tanzania
Cholera
Hepatitis A
Hepatitis B
Meningococcal meningitis
Typhoid
Yellow Fever

The yellow fever inoculation lasts 10 years and you are issued with a certificate. It is advisable when travelling to Kenya and Tanzania to carry the certificate with you. You cannot enter Tanzania or Kenya if you have travelled from an infected area without a certificate.

Rabies—many doctors advise that you have series of rabies jabs, but others do not. They are particularly expensive, so it may be wise to ask your doctor or nurse exactly what the facts are in relation to being protected against rabies.

It is recommended that when travelling to Kenya and Tanzania you are also covered for rubella, polio and mumps, and have boosters for diphtheria, measles and tetanus.

Medication

If you have any underlying medical problems, check that the drugs prescribed for you are legal in the country you are visiting. Take an up-to-date prescription with you, and sufficient medication to last the length of the trip and several weeks beyond the planned date of return. Important medication should be carried on your person at all times.

Malaria

Do not underestimate the dangers of contracting malaria—it kills between 1-3 million people every year (90% of them in Africa), and almost 2,000 UK residents return home each year having contracted malaria.

The practice nurse and pharmacist will advise on the appropriate anti-malarial medication. Malaria medication should be kept on your person at all times. No malarial medication is 100% effective, so take the following precautions:

Reduce the amount of skin exposed to mosquitoes by covering up from dusk to dawn—wear long trousers that go below the ankle, socks that go above the ankle, shoes (not sandals) and long-sleeved tops with a high neckline.

Clothing should be loose fitting and made from fabric with a close, tight weave.

Some outdoor clothing can be bought that is impregnated with a mosquito repellent.

Use a good insect repellent containing 50% DEET and apply regularly between dusk and dawn when mosquitoes and other insects are most active. The guides or locals will inform you if mosquitoes or tsetse flies are present. DEET comes either as a lotion, roll-on or spray. Spray-on DEET is useful if you have to apply this quickly.

Permethrin spray containing DEET is also useful for clothes and inside tents/rented rooms, as are plug-in insect vaporisers.

Always use mosquito nets when provided and make sure they are tucked underneath the bed.

No not leave lights on unnecessarily as they attract mosquitoes and other insects.

Do not wear perfume or aftershave as both attract mosquitoes and other insects.

Malaria Trivia

♦It is said that mosquitoes have a preference for biting people who wear the colour blue, have just eaten a banana, have just drunk alcohol or have smelly feet. They are also more likely to be attracted to a pregnant woman in preference to a non-pregnant one.

♦It is a myth that taking vitamin B, eating garlic and the use of ultrasonic devices will protect you from malaria.

♦Malaria is the world's second biggest killer after tuberculosis.

♦One child dies from malaria every 47 seconds.

<u>Although we are not medically qualified and therefore cannot technically recommend the following "first aid" items, they are all items that we have personally found to be very useful.</u>

Some form of medication for pain relief or if you have a fever.
Aspirin,paracetamol or Ibuprofen

Thermometer
A good indicator if you are developing malaria before you are aware of it.

Emergency Medical Kit
Emergency medical kit that includes a syringe, needles and scalpel Usually purchased from outdoor pursuits outlets and some pharmacies

Instruments
Swiss army knife, tweezers, scissors, magnifying glass, compact mirror and needles (to remove splinters).

Antibiotics
Ciprofloxacin 500mg is effective in treating infectious diarrhoea. This requires a private prescription.

Teeth
Dental fillings kit bought from pharmacies.
Toothache tincture or oil of cloves.

Eye care
Eye pad
Steripods that contain 20ml of sterile saline to wash the eye out.

195

Sickness & diarrhoea
Electrolyte replacement sachets.
Loperamide.

Open wounds/abrasions
Sterile gauze swabs (packs of 5).
Alcohol swabs.
Iodine spray (unless you are allergic to iodine).
Antiseptic cream.
Steri-strips for minor cuts.

Dressings
Cotton buds.
An assortment of wound dressings.
Silver plasters.
Plasters for blisters.

Bandages
Conforming bandages -
assorted sizes.
Micropore tape.
Plastic dressings for
abrasions-either "spray on"
or with an applicator.
Triangular bandages.

Chafed skin
Either Lanacane anti-chafing gel or Siopel.

Antihistamine tablets or cream
To be used for allergies, insect bites and stings.

Ticks
A tick twister to safely remove the body and head of a tick.

If you know that you are prone to other minor medical conditions, then take the appropriate medication along just in case. There is limited access to over the counter "first aid" in Kenya and Tanzania, and a minor ailment could spoil your holiday.

Prevention

Protection from the Sun-skin

A high factor, unscented sunscreen lotion.
Unscented aftersun cream.
Lip balm for dry, cracked lips.

Protection from the Sun–eyes

Good quality sun glasses that filter out harmful UVA and UVB rays.
Cap with a peak or brim to protect the eyes.

Chafed skin

Wear comfortable, good quality trousers that do not chafe the skin.

Blisters

Animal wool for prevention of blisters.

Water Purification

Water purification tablets, or iodine or chlorine tablets to sterilise water.

Sewing kit

Sewing kit (needles and thread) for repairs.

Bottled water for drinking.

Personal Care/Hygiene

Body/baby/face wipes.
Talc-not scented.
Antiperspirant–not scented.
Soap for personal use.
Household soap for washing clothes.
Good quality toilet paper.
Alcohol gel for hands (for general use and after toileting, to avoid stomach upsets).
Tissues or cotton handkerchiefs.
Ear plugs (campsites and townships can be particularly noisy right throughout the night).

Useful web sites

www.fco.gov.uk/travel
www.fitfortravel.nhs.uk
www.nathnac.org

Clothing

Going on safari is exciting, exhilarating and one enormous adventure. For many this will be a once in a lifetime holiday and for others who get the bug, the start of a lifelong relationship with East Africa. Regardless of whether you are staying in a luxury safari lodge, a tented camp site or actually camping in the bush, your safari will be expensive—probably your most expensive holiday ever.

Having spent so much of your hard-earned cash on a safari, you would not want to risk anything going wrong, and choosing the correct clothing is something that warrants careful consideration. Climatic conditions, exposure to the elements, environmental hazards, the lack of facilities, personal safety, personal hygiene and cultural respect require some thought with regard to the type of clothing that can be worn in environments that will certainly be new and testing for you.

If you have booked your safari through a tour operator they will give you some advice on type of clothing to be worn, but this is often cursory and superficial. It is worth thinking carefully about the type of clothing to be worn, as inappropriate clothing may well detract from what should be a pleasurable experience. Your clothes may need to be worn for several days without an opportunity to wash them, lack of facilities such as the availability of water (some lodges, guest houses and campsites will actually fine you for using water to wash clothes), the length of stay (which may not allow enough time for clothing to dry out), and luggage allowance (particularly on internal flights), may dictate the amount of clothing you can carry with you.

Do not wear expensive "fashionable" clothing when you are on safari as a combination of dust, perspiration, sun tan lotion, aftersun and insect repellents will soon discolour and spoil the fabric.

Cheap and functional safari type clothing can be bought on local market stalls, in some of the of the larger high street stores and online. Outdoor pursuit shops that specialise in outdoor clothing are worth investigating, but do tend to be expensive unless items are on special offer. If you have planned your safari well in advance you should have time to shop around for the best deals.

The major outdoor clothing manufacturers invest huge amounts of time and money in researching and developing high tech, high performance fabrics designed to cope with every environment you can imagine. The more properties a fabric incorporates the more it will cost. Be quite clear exactly what function you want the fabrics and the clothes to fulfil. What is important to you? What would spoil the safari experience for you?

The properties the fabrics may have are:

♦Stain resistant and water repellent. It is impossible to keep clothes clean on a safari, unless you close all your vehicle windows and turn on the air-conditioning—in which case you will probably miss most of the animals! Once you open the windows and viewing hatch you will soon be covered in dust, so fabrics that are stain resistant are a good idea. Depending on the time of year you may experience torrential rain, or if you are up early in the morning or walking through rain forests then clothing can get wet from the dew on the plants. You may be some time and distance away from your accommodation and will not have the opportunity to change clothes.

♦Thermal insulation. Despite being on the equator East Africa can be surprisingly cool at altitude, when there is overhead cloud cover, at dusk, dawn and during the night, particularly during the long dry season from June to October.

♦High temperatures during the middle of the day will cause the body to perspire and the increased wetness of the skin will add to bodily discomfort. Clothing made from natural fibres are not advisable as they retain moisture, can be chilly and cause skin chafing. Fibres with high wicking properties that draw moisture away from the body will add to bodily comfort.

♦Odour-resistant fibres impregnated with silver are effective in retarding and destroying microbes responsible for bodily odours—a significant problem when water for washing and personal hygiene may be scarce.

♦Clothes with sun-protective fibres that afford protection from the sun's harmful rays should be considered. The sun is extremely fierce over the equator, and a combination of altitude, cloud cover and low temperatures can be deceiving and lull you into a false sense of security. Do not underestimate how quickly the sun can burn and damage the skin.

♦Fast drying, minimum-iron fabrics allow more frequent changes of clothes.

♦Fibres impregnated with permanent insect repellents are highly effective against mosquitoes that spread malaria.

If you are buying new clothing, try them on before purchasing. You may be wearing them for several days so make sure they fit properly and are comfortable.

Clothing needs to:

♦Be lightweight and easily packed.

♦Be practical, comfortable and allow freedom of movement.

♦Have multiple zipped pockets for securing valuables (passports, money, credit cards and travellers cheques).

Suggested clothing

Safari jackets are recommended simply because of the number of pockets they have.

A warm fleece jacket is essential for the cold evenings.

Long trousers are a must for evenings and early mornings when the mosquitoes are most active, it they unzip and transform into shorts then even better as they can be used during the day

time. Multiple pockets with zips are needed to secure valuables and are more difficult for pickpockets to access. Long trousers should be worn when bush walking as they offer some degree of protection from sharp thorns, grasses that are razor sharp and from snake bites. Eighty per cent of venomous snake bites are to the lower leg, almost all of which occur at the ankle level. Trousers should go over the ankle.

Shorts with multiple zipped pockets.

Long-sleeved tops are required from dusk until dawn when the mosquitoes are active. Tops with a zipped up neck and cuffs will further deter these unwelcome visitors. It is possible to buy shirts with sleeves that roll up and are held in place by a buttoned flap, or that completely unzip from the body of the shirt.

Socks that cover the ankles for use on an evening.

Trainers or sandals for inside your safari vehicle, in lodges and in campsites, but do not wear sandals in the evening or if you are walking in the bush.

A wide-brimmed hat or peaked cap to protect the eyes.

Thermals or pyjamas are necessary when camping in the long dry season when it is particularly cool at night.

Trivia

◆If you intend to walk about in the cities, towns and villages do not wear new, expensive fashionable clothing as this immediately draws attention to yourself—the perception is that you are a wealthy tourist on holiday. It is far better to wear old clothes that fully cover the arms and legs and allow you to blend in with the locals.

◆Clothing should be made from fabrics that have a tight weave and they should be loose fitting—this makes it more difficult for insects to bite you (particularly the tsetse fly, which can carry sleeping sickness).

◆Clothes should be neutral and blend in with the background when you are on game drives–khaki type colours will not be visually offensive to the animals.

◆Avoid wearing blue as it has been proved that this attracts mosquitoes.

Republic of Kenya

Kenya is a large country on the east coast of Africa lying from 4° north to 4° south of the equator and between 34° and 41° east of the Greenwich Meridian. It borders with Somalia, Ethiopia, Sudan, Uganda, Tanzania and the Indian Ocean.

Official name The Republic of Kenya
Government Republic
Area 582,650 sq km
Terrain Semi-desert, savannahs and tropical rainforests
Climate Tropical along the coast, arid interior.
Capital Nairobi
Population 39.8 million (2009). 70 tribal groups. Main ethnic groups: Ameru, Embu, Kikuyu, Luhya, Luo, Kalenjin, Kamba, Kissii, Maasai, Meru, Taita and Turkana.
Life expectancy 55 years (men and women).
Languages Kiswahili, English, numerous indigenous languages.
Major religions Christianity (Protestant), Roman Catholic, Islam and indigenous beliefs.
Monetary Kenyan shilling
Main industries Agriculture, beer, cement, chemicals, clothing, electrical equipment, food processing, flowers, leather goods, oil refining, publishing & printing, rubber, textiles, tourism, wood & cork products.
Main trading partners UK, Germany, Iran, Japan, Netherlands, Saudi Arabia, Tanzania, USA and Zambia.
Major markets UK, Netherlands, Uganda, Tanzania,Pakistan and USA.
Main exports Cassava, cement, coffee, cotton, fish, fruit, horticultural products (flowers and vegetables), leather, maize, millet, nuts, petroleum products, shell fish, sisal, spices, sweet potatoes, tea, tobacco, tourism.
Natural hazards Drought, recurrent floods during the rainy seasons.
Environmental issues Water pollution, soil degradation, deforestation, desertification, soil erosion & poaching.
Time GMT +3
International dialling code +254 or 00 254
Climate
Although Kenya is an equatorial country, it does not have an equatorial climate and this is attributed to altitude, the nature of the terrain, the winds and distance from the sea. Most of Kenya is 1,200m above sea level and this dissipates the heat.

Kenya has a pleasant, tropical climate, and is warm and sunny throughout the year. Day and night are equal. The sun rises at 6.15 a.m. and sets at 6.45 p.m. every day. Temperatures range from warm to hot at midday and evenings, and early mornings are usually cool.

The climate on the coast is tropical and is consistently hot and humid. Temperatures at midday rise to 30°C and fall to 15°C on an evening. Rainfall is 110cm per annum.

Inland, on the plateau and the highlands where the altitude is between 1,200-2,200m above sea level the climate is temperate. Temperatures on the interior are 25°C at mid day and fall to 10°C on an evening with annual rainfall that ranges between 170-190cm.

The climate is humid around Lake Victoria due to the presence of moist winds rising from the lake. Temperatures are between 22-33°C during the day and can fall to 17°C on an evening. Average rainfall ranges are between 170-195cm per annum.

The arid and semi-arid bush lands of northern and north eastern Kenya are extremely hot and very dry with temperatures reaching 40°C+ during the day and falling to 20°C on an evening. Rainfall is 35cm per annum. This is a remote and inhospitable environment that is home to a few hardy nomads.

Mountainous areas above 2,500m have a much colder climate. Frost may be present on a morning and permanent snow on the higher slopes.

Kenya has alternating long and short rainy seasons and long and short dry seasons that are affected by the position and movement of the overhead sun. The cool, dry seasons occur when the sun is overhead in the opposite hemisphere and the hot, wet seasons occur when the sun has returned to the overhead position.

Rainy seasons

The long rainy season is from March to June and is characterised by regular, torrential downpours and violent storms in the morning and at night. The rainy season is sometimes referred to as the green season, as all the vegetation springs back to life. The short rainy season is from early October to December and is characterised by light showers in the morning and late afternoon.

Dry seasons

The long, dry season is from June to October and is the winter season. It is usually overcast and is the coolest and most pleasant time of the year. The short, dry season is from December to March and is the hottest and driest time of the year.

The highlands of western Kenya have a single rainy season from March through to September.

203

Trivia

♦The word *Kenya* means "white mountain".

♦Mt Kenya is an extinct volcano and at 5,199m is the highest mountain in Kenya.

♦The main lakes in Kenya are: Baringo, Bogoria, Elementeita, Naivasha, Nakuru, Magadi, Turkana and Victoria.

♦Lake Victoria is Africa's largest lake. It covers 70,000 sq km.

♦Kenya shares Lake Victoria with Tanzania and Uganda.

♦The Kibera slum, in Nairobi, is the largest slum in Africa. Up to one million people live there and 50% are under the age of 15.

♦In Kenya, 2.2 million people are HIV positive. 700 Kenyans die of AIDS every day.

♦50% of the population in Kenya lives below the poverty line.

List of Kenyan National Parks, Game Reserves, Private Conservancies, Wildlife Sanctuaries and Trusts.

Aberdare National Park
Amboseli National Park
Arabuko Sokoke National Reserve
Arawale National Reserve
Bisanandi National Reserve
Boni National Reserve
Buffalo Springs National Reserve
Central Highlands National Park
Chyulu Hills National Park
Diani/Chale Marine National Park and Reserve
Dodori National Reserve
El Karama Ranch/Reserve
Hells Gate National Park
Kakamega Forest National Reserve
Kerio Valley/Lake Kamnarok National Reserve
Kisite Marine National Park
Kiunga Marine National Reserve
Kora National Park
Laikipia Plateau Park/Reserve
Lake Baringo National Reserve
Lake Bogoria National Reserve
Lake Nakuru National Park
Losai National Reserve
Maasai Mara National Reserve
Malindi Marine National Park
Mara Triangle (North western part of Maasai Mara)
Marsabit National Park & Reserve

Meru National Park
Mombasa Marine National Park & Reserve
Mkogodo Forest Reserve
Mpunguti Marine National Park & Reserve
Mt Elgon National Park
Mt Kenya National Park
Mt Longonot National Park
Mwea National Reserve
Mwingi National Reserve (formerly North Kitui National Reserve)
Nairobi National Park
Ngai Ndethya National Reserve
Nasolot National Reserve
Ndere Island National Park
Ol Donyo Sabuk National Park
Rahole National Reserve
Ruma National Park
Saiwa Swamp National Park
Samburu National Reserve
Shaba National Reserve
Shimba Hills National Reserve
Sibiloi National Park
Solio Game Reserve
South Islands National Park
South Kitui National Reserve
South Turkana National Reserve
Tana River Primate Reserve
Tsavo East National Park
Tsavo West National Park
Watamu Marine National Park

Kenya
Wildlife Sanctuaries, Conservancies & Trusts

Bio Ken Snake Farm & Laboratory
Crater Lake Sanctuary
Crescent Island Wildlife Sanctuary
David Sheldrick Wildlife Trust
Elsamere Conservation Centre
Haller Park
Impala Sanctuary
Kigio Wildlife Conservancy
Kimana Wildlife Sanctuary
Kipini Wildlife & Botanical Conservancy
Kisuma Bird Sanctuary

Kisuma Impala Wildlife Sanctuary
Lewa Wildlife Conservancy
Lumo Community Wildlife Sanctuary
Malinda Crocodile & Snake Park
Maralal Game Sanctuary
Mida Creek
Mwaluganje Elephant Sanctuary
Nairobi Animal Orphanage
Nairobi Safari Walk
Ngare Sergoi Rhino Sanctuary
Ngulia Rhino Sanctuary
Nguuni Wildlife Sanctuary
Ol Pejeta Conservancy
Oserian Wildlife Sanctuary (formerly Kongoni Game Sanctuary)
Rukinga Wildlife Conservancy
Shampole Conservancy
Sweetwaters Game Reserve and Chimpanzee Sanctuary
Taita Hills Wildlife Sanctuary

Kenyan National Parks and Reserves—Wildlife
Aberdare National Park
African wild dog (also known as African hunting dog), baboon, bongo, bush pig, Cape buffalo, colobus monkey, dik-dik, duiker, eland, elephant, Grant's gazelle, genet cat, giant forest hog, giraffe, golden cat, hyena, impala, leopard, lion, reedbuck, rhinoceros (black & white), serval cat, suni, Sykes' monkey, Thomson's gazelle, vervet monkey, vulture, warthog and waterbuck.

Amboseli National Park
Aardwolf, African wild dog, antelope, baboon, bat-eared fox, bushbaby, bushbuck, Cape buffalo, caracal, cheetah, civet cat, dik-dik, duiker, eland, elephant, gerenuk, genet cat, giraffe, Grant's gazelle, hare, hartebeest (also known as kongoni), hippopotamus, honey badger (also known as ratel), hyena, hyrax, impala, jackal, klipspringer, kudu, leopard, lesser flamingo, lion, mongoose, oryx, porcupine, reedbuck, rhinoceros (black & white), serval cat, steinbok, Sykes' monkey, Thomson's gazelle, vervet monkey, waterbuck, wildebeest, zebra, and zorilla (also known as striped pole cat).

Arabuko Sokoke National Reserve
Aardvark, baboon, boomslang, bushbaby, bushbuck, Cape buffalo, caracal, chameleon, civet cat, duiker, eland, elephant, genet cat, golden rumped elephant shrew, green mamba, red bush squirrel, rock python, mongoose, Sykes' monkey, suni, Thomson's gazelle, vervet monkey, waterbuck and zebra.

Arawale National Reserve
African wild dog, Cape buffalo, caracal, cheetah, crocodile, dik-dik, duiker, eland, elephant, giraffe, Grant's gazelle, hartebeest, hippopotamus, honey badger, hyena, jackal, kudu, oryx, topi, vervet monkey, warthog and zebra.

Bisanandi National Reserve
Cape buffalo, cheetah, elephant, giraffe, hippopotamus, lion and rhinoceros.

Boni National Reserve
Aardwolf, African wild dog, bush pig, Cape buffalo, duiker, elephant, gerenuk, giraffe, hippopotamus, topi, vulture, warthog and waterbuck.

Buffalo Springs National Reserve
African wild dog, Cape buffalo, cheetah, crocodile (Nile), dik-dik, eland, elephant, gerenuk, giraffe, Grant's gazelle, hippopotamus, hyena, impala, kudu, leopard, lion, oryx, ostrich, warthog, waterbuck and zebra.

Central Islands National Park
Giraffe, Grant's gazelle, hippopotamus, oryx, topi and zebra.

Chyulu Hills National Park
African wild dog, antelope, baboon, black mamba, bushbuck, Cape buffalo, cheetah, crocodile, dik-dik, eland, elephant, gerenuk, giant forest hog, giraffe, Grant's gazelle, hartebeest, hyena, hyrax, impala, klipspringer, kudu, leopard, lion, mongoose, oryx, puff adder, python, reedbuck, rhinoceros (black), steinbok, Thomson's gazelle, tortoise, vulture, warthog, waterbuck, wildebeest and zebra.

Dodori National Reserve
Antelope, elephant, gazelle, giraffe, hippopotamus, kudu, lion and topi.

El Karama Ranch/Reserve
African wild dog, Cape buffalo, cheetah, elephant, giraffe, hartebeest, hippopotamus, hyena, impala, lion, leopard, oryx and Grevy's zebra.

Hells Gate National Park
African hare, African wild dog, African wild cat, antelope, baboon, bat-eared fox, bushbuck, Cape buffalo, caracal, cheetah, civet cat, colobus monkey, dik-dik, duiker, eland, genet cat, giraffe, Grant's gazelle, hartebeest, honey badger, hyena, hyrax, impala, jackal, klipspringer, leopard, lion, mongoose, porcupine, reedbuck, serval cat, steinbok, Thomson's gazelle, vervet monkey, warthog, wildebeest and zebra.

Kakamega Forest National Reserve
Aardvark, baboon, bushbaby, bush pig, Cape buffalo, civet cat, clawless otter, colobus monkey, De Brazza monkey, dik-dik, duiker, East African hedgehog, forest cobra, forest pig, Gabon viper, giant

forest squirrel, giant rat, giant water shrew, giraffe, Grant's gazelle, hartebeest, hippopotamus, hyena, jackal, Jameson's mamba, leopard, mongoose, red tailed monkey, roan antelope, serval cat, suni, Sykes' monkey, pangolin, porcupine, reedbuck, rhinoceros viper, Thomson's gazelle, water shrew and vervet monkey.

Kerio Valley/Lake Kamnarok National Reserve
Antelope, bush pig, Cape buffalo, crocodile, dik-dik, elephant, gazelle, giraffe, impala, leopard, ostrich, warthog and waterbuck.

Kora National Reserve
Antelope, Cape buffalo, dik-dik, elephant, giraffe, Grant's gazelle, hippopotamus, leopard, lion, oryx, serval cat and zebra.

Laikipia Plateau Park/Reserve
African wild dog, antelope, Cape buffalo, cheetah, elephant, gazelle, gerenuk, giraffe, Grant's gazelle, hartebeest, hippopotamus, hyena, impala, leopard, lion, oryx, ostrich, rhinoceros (black & white), sitatunga antelope, Thomson's gazelle and zebra.

Lake Baringo National Reserve
African fish eagle, crocodile, flamingo, hippopotamus, marabou stork and monitor lizard.

Lake Bogoria National Reserve
Baboon, Cape buffalo, caracal, cheetah, dik-dik, flamingo, Grant's gazelle, hyena, impala, klipspringer, kudu, monkey, reedbuck, Thomson's gazelle, warthog and zebra.

Lake Nakuru National Park
African wild cat, baboon, bat-eared fox, bushbuck, Cape buffalo, colobus monkey, dik-dik, duiker, eland, flamingo, giraffe, golden cat, Grant's gazelle, hare, hartebeest, hippopotamus, hyena, hyrax, impala, jackal, klipspringer, leopard, lion, long eared leaf nosed bat, mongoose, python, reedbuck, rhinoceros (black & white), steinbok, Thomson's gazelle, vervet monkey, warthog, waterbuck and zebra.

Losai National Reserve
Cobra, elephant, gerenuk, Grant's gazelle, kudu, python and rhinoceros (black).

Maasai Mara National Reserve
Baboon, bat-eared fox, Cape buffalo, cheetah, crocodile, dik-dik, eland, elephant, giraffe, Grant's gazelle, hartebeest, hippopotamus, hyena, hyrax, impala, jackal, leopard, lion, oribi, ostrich, roan antelope, rhinoceros (black & white), Thomson's gazelle, topi, vulture, warthog, waterbuck, wildebeest and zebra.

Mara Triangle (North-western part of the Maasai Mara)
Baboon, bat-eared fox, Cape buffalo, cheetah, crocodile, elephant, Grant's gazelle, hyena, hippopotamus, impala, jackal, leopard, lion, rhinoceros, Thomson's gazelle, warthog, waterbuck and zebra.

Marsabit National Park & Reserve
Aardwolf, antelope, baboon, bushbuck, Cape buffalo, caracal, cheetah, dik-dik, elephant, giraffe, Grant's gazelle, hyena, klipspringer, kudu, leopard, lion, monkey, oryx, rhinoceros (black), warthog, waterbuck and zebra.

Meru National Park
African wild dog, antelope, baboon, bushbuck, bushbaby, bush pig, Cape buffalo, caracal, cheetah, civet cat, crocodile, cobra, dik-dik, duiker, eland, elephant, genet cat, gerenuk, giraffe, hartebeest, hippopotamus, hyena, hyrax, impala, jackal, leopard, lion, kudu, mongoose, oribi, oryx, ostrich, porcupine, python, puff adder, serval cat, reedbuck, rhinoceros (black & white), vervet monkey, warthog, waterbuck, wild cat and zebra.

Mkogodo Forest Reserve
Bushbuck, bush pig, Cape buffalo, cheetah, duiker, eland, elephant, gerenuk, leopard, lion and zebra.

Mt Elgon National Park
Antelope, blue monkey, bushbuck, Cape buffalo, civet cat, colobus monkey, De Brazza monkey, duiker, elephant, forest monkey, giant forest hog, golden cat, hyena, hyrax, impala, jackal, leopard, oribi, tree squirrel, reedbuck, waterbuck and wild cat.

Mt Kenya National Park
Antelope, baboon, blue monkey, bongo, bushbuck, bush pig, Cape buffalo, civet cat, colobus monkey, duiker, eland, elephant, giant forest hog, genet cat, forest monkey, hyena, hyrax, jackal, leopard, lion, mongoose, Montane viper, Mt Kenya mole shrew, oribi, reedbuck, rhinoceros (black), hyrax, serval cat, skink, suni, Sykes' monkey, tree squirrel, waterbuck, wild cat and zebra.

Mt Longonot National Park
Antelope, baboon, bushbuck, Cape buffalo, cheetah, colobus monkey, eland, Grant's gazelle, hartebeest, impala, leopard, lion, Thomson's gazelle, vervet monkey and zebra.

Mwea National Reserve
Aardvark, baboon, bushbuck, bush pig, Cape buffalo, crocodile, dik-dik, duiker, eland, elephant, genet cat, giraffe, ground squirrel, hartebeest, hippopotamus, hyena, hyrax, impala, jackal, kudu, leopard, lion, mongoose, porcupine, serval cat, Sykes' monkey, tortoise, vervet monkey, warthog, waterbuck and zebra.

Mwingi National Reserve (formerly North Kitui National Reserve)
Antelope, Cape buffalo, caracal, crocodile, elephant, hippopotamus, leopard, lion and warthog.

Nairobi National Park

Antelope, baboon, bushbuck, Cape buffalo, cheetah, crocodile, dik-dik, eland, gerenuk, giraffe, Grant's gazelle, hartebeest, hippopotamus, hyena, hyrax, impala, jackal, klipspringer, leopard, lion, monkey, ostrich, reedbuck, rhinoceros (black & white), Thomson's gazelle, vulture, warthog, waterbuck, wildebeest and zebra

Ngai Ndethya National Reserve

Cape buffalo, elephant and kudu.

Nasolot National Reserve

Baboon, Cape buffalo, dik-dik, duiker, eland, elephant, gazelle, hippopotamus, hyena, jackal, impala, kudu, leopard, lion, oryx, Sykes' monkey, waterbuck and zebra.

Ndere Island National Park

Baboon, crocodile, hippopotamus, impala, monitor lizard, sitatunga antelope and vervet monkey.

Ol Donyo Sabuk National Park

Aardvark, baboon, bushbaby, bushbuck, bush pig, Cape buffalo, colobus monkey, dik-dik, duiker, ground squirrel, hartebeest, hyrax, impala, jackal, kudu, leopard, mongoose, monitor lizard, monkey, porcupine, python, reedbuck, rhinoceros (black), Sykes' monkey, vervet monkey, vulture and waterbuck.

Rahole National Reserve

Crocodile, elephant, hippopotamus, oryx and zebra.

Ruma National Park (formerly Lambwe Valley National Reserve)

Aardvark, African hare, African spitting cobra, African wild cat, agama, baboon, cane cat, Cape buffalo, cheetah, bushbuck, chimpanzee, gazelle, genet cat, giraffe, hartebeest, hyena, impala, leopard, lion, mongoose, oribi, ostrich, otter, porcupine, puff adder, reedbuck, roan antelope, serval cat, steinbok, topi, vervet monkey, vulture, waterbuck and zebra.

Saiwa Swamp National Park

Blue monkey, bushbuck, colobus monkey, De Brazza monkey, duiker, genet cat, giant forest squirrel, honey badger, leopard, mongoose, otter, potto, sitatunga antelope, serval cat, vervet monkey and vulture.

Samburu National Reserve

Cape buffalo, cheetah, crocodile, dik-dik, eland, elephant, gerenuk, giraffe, Grant's gazelle, hartebeest, hippopotamus, hyena, kudu, impala, leopard, lion, oryx, ostrich, rhinoceros (black & white), warthog, waterbuck and zebra.

Shaba National Reserve

Cape buffalo, cheetah, crocodile, dik-dik, elephant, giraffe, gerenuk, Grant's gazelle, hippopotamus, kudu, leopard, lion, oryx, ostrich, waterbuck and zebra.

Shimba Hills National Reserve

Baboon, black and red shrew, bushbaby, bushbuck, bush pig, elephant, Cape buffalo, cheetah, civet cat, colobus monkey, duiker, giraffe, hyena, leopard, lion, ostrich, reedbuck, roan antelope, sable antelope, serval cat, Sykes' monkey, vervet monkey, vulture, warthog and waterbuck.

Sibiloi National Park

Cheetah, crocodile, gerenuk, giraffe, Grant's gazelle, hippopotamus, hyena, jackal, kudu, leopard, lion, oribi, oryx, ostrich, topi, vulture and zebra.

Solio Game Reserve

Cape buffalo, cheetah, colobus monkey, eland, gazelle, giraffe, hartebeest, leopard, lion, oryx, rhinoceros (black & white) and zebra.

South Islands & Central National Park

Cobra, crocodile, flamingo, giraffe, Grant's gazelle, hippopotamus, kudu, night adder, oryx, pelican, puff adder, topi and zebra.

South Kitui National Reserve

Baboon, Cape buffalo, cheetah, dik-dik, eland, elephant, gazelle, gemsbok, gerenuk, giraffe, hartebeest, hippopotamus, kudu, leopard, lion, oryx, rhinoceros, waterbuck and zebra.

South Turkana National Reserve

Cape buffalo, bushbuck, cheetah, crocodile, eland, elephant, giraffe, Grant's gazelle, hippopotamus, hyena, impala, jackal, kudu, leopard, lion, oryx, Thomson's gazelle, topi and zebra.

Tana River Primate Reserve

Antelope, baboon, bushbaby, bushbuck, Cape buffalo, caracal, cheetah, colobus monkey, crocodile, forest pig, giraffe, gazelle, gerenuk, hartebeest, hippopotamus, hyena, impala, kudu, leopard, lion, mangabey, monitor lizard, oryx, python, red colobus monkey, vervet monkey, waterbuck and zebra.

Tsavo East National Park

Aardwolf, African dormouse, African hare, African wild dog, African wild cat, baboon, bat-eared fox, bushbaby, bushbuck, bush squirrel, Cape buffalo, caracal, cheetah, civet cat, crocodile, dik-dik, duiker, East African hedgehog, eland, elephant, elephant shrew, gazelle, genet cat, gerenuk, giraffe, hartebeest, hippopotamus, hyena, impala, jackal, klipspringer, kudu, leopard, lion, mongoose, oryx, ostrich, pangolin, porcupine, reedbuck, rhinoceros (black), serval cat, suni, Sykes' monkey, vervet monkey, vulture, warthog, waterbuck and zebra.

Tsavo West National Park

Aardwolf, African wild dog, antelope, baboon, bushbuck, Cape buffalo, caracal, cheetah, crocodile, dik-dik, duiker, eland, elephant, gazelle, gerenuk, giraffe, ground squirrel, hartebeest, hippopotamus, hyena, hyrax, impala, klipspringer, kudu, leopard, lion, mongoose, oryx, rhinoceros (black), serval cat, steinbok, suni, vulture, warthog, waterbuck, wildebeest and zebra.

Kenyan Wildlife Sanctuaries, Conservancies and Trusts— Wildlife

Bio Ken Snake Farm & Laboratory

Bio Ken Snake Farm & Laboratory is a medical research centre that is also involved in the preparation of antivenom. Visitors to the centre can view venomous and non-venomous snakes.

Crater Lake Game Sanctuary

Baboon, Cape buffalo, colobus monkey, eland, flamingo, gazelle, giraffe, hartebeest, warthog and zebra.

Crescent Island Wildlife Sanctuary

Eland, giraffe, Grant's gazelle, impala, python, Thomson's gazelle, waterbuck and wildebeest.

David Sheldrick Wildlife Trust

Orphaned elephants and rhinoceros.

Elsamere Conservation Centre

Colobus monkey and hippopotamus.

Haller Park

Antelope, bushbuck, bush pig, Cape buffalo, crocodile, duiker, eland, giraffe, hippopotamus, mongoose, oryx, ostrich, porcupine, serval cat, sitatunga antelope, suni, Sykes' monkey, vervet monkey, waterbuck and zebra.

Kigio Wildlife Conservancy

Antelope, Cape buffalo, eland, giraffe, Grant's gazelle, hippopotamus, hyena, impala, leopard, python, Thomson's gazelle and zebra.

Kimana Wildlife Sanctuary

Cape buffalo, eland, gazelle, giraffe, hippopotamus, leopard and lion.

Kipini Wildlife & Botanical Conservancy

African wild dog, Cape buffalo, colobus monkey, cheetah, gerenuk, giraffe, hippopotamus, hyena, kudu, leopard, lion, Sykes' monkey, topi, vervet monkey, warthog and zebra.

Kisuma Bird Sanctuary

An area of swampland that is rich in bird life and is a breeding ground for storks, cormorants and egrets.

Kisuma Impala Wildlife Sanctuary

Baboon, hippopotamus, hyena, jackal, impala, leopard, ostrich, vervet monkey and vulture.

Lewa Wildlife Conservancy

Cape buffalo, eland, elephant, giraffe, impala, leopard, lion, oryx, rhinoceros (black & white), sitatunga antelope, waterbuck and zebra.

Lumo Community Wildlife Sanctuary

Aardvark, African wildcat, antelope, baboon, bat-eared fox, bushbuck, bush squirrel, caracal, Cape buffalo, cheetah, civet cat, crocodile, dik-dik, duiker, eland, elephant, gazelle, genet cat, giraffe, ground squirrel, hartebeest, hedgehog, honey badger, hyena, hyrax, impala, jackal, klipspringer, kudu, leopard, lion, mole rat, mongoose, monitor lizard, oryx, porcupine, reedbuck, serval cat, steinbok, suni, vervet monkey, waterbuck, zebra and zorilla.

Maralal Game Sanctuary

Baboon, bushbuck, bush pig, Cape buffalo, cheetah, duiker, eland, elephant, gerenuk, hyena, impala, leopard, lion, warthog and zebra.

Mwaluganje Elephant Sanctuary

Baboon, bushbuck, colobus monkey, elephant, jackal, leopard, monkey, Sykes' monkey, waterbuck, warthog and zebra.

Nairobi Animal Orphanage

Nairobi Animal Orphanage is located in the grounds of Nairobi National Park.

Baboon, Cape buffalo, caracal, cheetah, crocodile, duiker, hyena, jackal, leopard, lion, mongoose, ostrich, patas monkey, serval cat, Sokoke forest cat, tortoise and warthog.

Nairobi Safari Walk

Nairobi Safari Walk is located in the grounds of Nairobi National Park.

Antelope, baboon, bongo, Cape buffalo, cheetah, colobus monkey, crocodile, gazelle, giraffe, hippopotamus, hyena, leopard, lion, ostrich, oryx, rhinoceros (white), tortoise, wildebeest and zebra.

Ngare Sergoi Rhino Sanctuary (extended in 1992 to incorporate Lewa Downs Ranch)

Rhinoceros (black & white).

Ngulia Rhino Sanctuary

Rhinoceros (black).

Nguuni Wildlife Sanctuary

Camel, eland, giraffe, oryx, ostrich and waterbuck.

Ol Pejeta Conservancy (formerly known as Sweetwaters)

Aardvark, aardwolf, African wild cat, baboon, bushbaby, bush squirrel, Cape buffalo, caracal, cheetah, civet cat, crocodile, duiker, eland, elephant, elephant shrew, genet cat, giraffe, Grant's gazelle, hare, hartebeest, hippopotamus, honey badger, hyena, hyrax, impala, jackal, kudu, leopard, lion, mongooses oryx, ostrich, otter, patas monkey, porcupine, reedbuck, rhinoceros (black & white), serval cat, steinbok, suni, Thomson's gazelle, vervet monkey, warthog, waterbuck, zebra and zorilla.

Oserian Wildlife Sanctuary (formerly Kongoni Game Sanctuary)

Aardvark, African wild dog, antelope, Cape buffalo, cheetah dik-dik, giraffe, hippopotamus, kudu, leopard, lion, oryx, ostrich, rhinoceros (white) topi, wildebeest, zebra (Grevy's) and zorilla.

Rukinga Wildlife Conservancy

Aardvark, African wild dog, African wild cat, agama, baboon, bat-eared fox, black mamba, boomslang, bush pig, Cape buffalo, caracal, chameleon, cheetah, civet cat, cobra, dik-dik, duiker, eland, elephant, genet cat, gerenuk, giraffe, Grant's gazelle, hartebeest, honey badger, hyena, hyrax, impala, jackal, klipspringer, kudu, leopard, lion, mongoose, puff adder, python, serval cat, tortoise, vervet monkey, warthog, waterbuck, zebra and zorilla.

Shampole Conservancy

Aardwolf, African wild dog, anteater, antelope, baboon, bat-eared fox, cheetah, civet cat, eland, giraffe, hippopotamus, hyena, leopard, lion, monkey, oryx, ostrich, python, serval cat and zebra.

Sweetwaters Game Reserve & Chimpanzee Sanctuary (currently part of Ol Pejeta Conservancy and detailed in that section)

Taita Hills Wildlife Sanctuary

Black-backed jackal, bushbaby, bushbuck, Cape buffalo, cheetah, civet cat, eland, elephant, genet cat, giraffe, Grant's gazelle, hartebeest, honey badger, hyena, kudu, leopard, lion, mongoose, oryx, porcupine, reedbuck, waterbuck and zebra.

United Republic of Tanzania

Tanzania is the largest country in East Africa lying from 1° to 11° south of the equator and between 30° and 40° east of the Greenwich Meridian. It borders with Kenya, Uganda, Rwanda, Burundi, Democratic Republic of the Congo, Zambia, Malawi, Mozambique and the Indian Ocean.

Official name United Republic of Tanzania
Government Republic
Area 945,00 sq km
Terrain Plains along the coast. Central Plateau. Highlands, north & south.
Climate Tropical along the coast and temperate in the Highlands
Capital Dodoma (Administrative) Dar-Es-Salaam (Commercial)
Population 41 million (2009). 99% of the population are black Africans. There are 130 ethnic groups. The five main ethnic groups are: Bantu, Nilotic, Nilo-Hamitic, Khoisan and Iraqw.
Language Kiswahili, English, Arabic & 100 local languages.
Major religions Christianity (34%), Islam (33%), remainder follow local tribal beliefs.
Life expectancy 55 years (men), 56 years (women)
49% of the population is under 15 years old.
Monetary Tanzanian shilling
Natural resources Coal, diamonds, gemstones, gold, iron ore, natural gas, nickel, phosphates and tin.
Main industries Agriculture, cement, food processing, oil refining and textiles.
Main trading partners UK, Bahrain, China, Germany, Indonesia, Italy, Japan, Malaysia, Pakistan, Singapore, South Korea and Thailand.
Major markets UK, Germany, India, Italy and Japan.
Food production Bananas, cashew nuts, cocoa beans, coffee, maize, millet, sugar cane, sorghum and rice.
Main exports Cashew nuts, cloves, coconuts, coffee, cotton, cut flowers, fish, minerals (gold, diamonds, gemstones), seaweed, sisal, tea and tobacco.
Natural hazards Tsetse flies. Drought. Floods in the Central Plateau during the rainy season.
Environmental issues Soil degradation, deforestation, desertification, destruction of coral reefs and recent droughts.
Time GMT +3
International dialling codes +255 or 00 255

Climate

Tanzania lies just south of the equator, as a result there is very little seasonal variation in temperature with the climate being warm and pleasant all year round.

Tanzania is a large country and the climate ranges from tropical to temperate and is heavily influenced by altitude, the nature of the terrain and distance from the sea. There is usually between seven to ten hours of sunshine per day and the evenings are cool. Temperatures, rainfall and humidity decrease as you move inland with the increasing altitude. Annual rainfall is between 50-100cm.

The majority of Tanzania enjoys a tropical climate but at altitudes of 900m+ there is a significant reduction in temperature that is very noticeable at night, when temperatures in the mountainous regions may fall below freezing.

The coastal region, including the islands of Mafia, Pemba and Zanzibar, has a tropical climate. It is hot with average daytime temperatures between 27-30°C. Humidity is high, although sea breezes have a cooling effect and make oppressive climatic conditions bearable. Coastal areas receive rain during most months. Annual rainfall on the coast is between 100-150cm.

The central plateau has a semi-arid climate and has high daytime temperatures and cool evenings. Average daytime temperatures range between 19°-27°C depending on the time of year. Annual rainfall is less than 57cm.

The north-eastern and southern areas are cool, having a semi-temperate climate and average temperatures range between 15-21°C.

Central, northern and western Tanzania's climate is modified by the high plateau. Humidity is lower and temperatures range from 20-27°C in the cooler months and may be as high as 30°C between December and March.

Northern Tanzania has two rainy seasons and two dry seasons. The rainy seasons can vary slightly from area to area.

The long rainy season or *Masika* is from March to June and is characterised by regular, torrential afternoon downpours and violent storms. The short rainy season *Vuli* is from November to December and is characterised by light sporadic showers.

The long dry season is from June to October and is the coolest time of the year. Temperature varies with altitude and can fall below freezing in areas such as the rim of the Ngorongoro Crater and on the slopes of Kilimanjaro and Mt Meru. The short dry season is from January to February and is the hottest time of the year.

The rest of the country has one wet season from November to May.

Trivia

♦The lowest point in Tanzania is the Indian Ocean.

♦At 5,890m Kilimanjaro is the highest mountain in Africa, and the world's highest free-standing mountain.

♦Lake Victoria is the world's second largest freshwater lake.

♦Lake Tanganyika is the world's second deepest lake.

♦58% of the population live on less than one US Dollar per day.

♦38% of the children in Tanzania are chronically malnourished.

List of Tanzanian National Parks and Game Reserves

Arusha National Park
Biharamulo Game Reserve
Burigi Game Reserve
Gombe Stream National Park
Ibanda Game Reserve
Jozani Chwaka Bay National Park
Katavi National Park
Kigosi & Moyowasi Game Reserve
Kitulo Plateau National Park
Kizigo Game Reserve
Lake Manyara National Park
Lukwika-Lumesule Game Reserve
Mafia Island Marine Park
Mahale Mountains National Park
Maswa Game Reserve
Mikumi National Park
Mkomazi Game Reserve
Mnazi Bay Ruvumba Estuary Marine Park
Msangesi Game Reserve
Muhesi Game Reserve
Mt Kilimanjaro National Park
Ngezi Forest Reserve
Ngorongoro Conservation Area
Ruaha National Park
Rubondo Island National Park
Rumanyika Game Reserve
Rungwa Game Reserve
Saa Nane Game Reserve
Saadani National Park
Selous Game Reserve
Serengeti National Park
Tarangire National Park
Udzungwa Mountains National Park

Ugalla River Game Reserve
Umba River Game Reserve
Uwanda Game Reserve

Tanzanian National Parks and Reserves—List of Wildlife
Arusha National Park
Antelope, baboon, blue monkey, bushbuck, Cape buffalo, colobus monkey, dik-dik, duiker, elephant flamingo, giraffe, hippopotamus, hyena, leopard, reedbuck, warthog, waterbuck and zebra.
Biharamulo Game Reserve
Buffalo, colobus monkey, crocodile, eland, elephant, hartebeest, hippopotamus, impala, reedbuck, roan antelope, rhinoceros, sable antelope, steinbok, sitatunga antelope, topi, waterbuck and zebra.
Burigi Game Reserve
Cape buffalo, bushbuck, duiker, eland, elephant, giraffe, hippopotamus, impala, klipspringer, lion, oribi, reedbuck, roan antelope, sable antelope, sitatunga antelope, steinbok, topi, warthog, waterbuck and zebra.
Gombe Stream National Park
Baboon, black mamba, blue monkey, boomslang, bushbaby, bushbuck, bush pig, cane rat, Cape buffalo, chimpanzee, civet cat, colobus monkey, elephant shrew, forest bush pig, genet cat, hippopotamus, hyena, leopard, lion, mongoose, monitor lizard, pangolin, puff adder, python, red tailed monkey, serval cat, tree squirrel and vervet monkey.
Ibanda Game Reserve
Cape buffalo, eland, elephant, giraffe, hippopotamus, impala, reedbuck, roan antelope, sable antelope, sitatunga antelope, topi, warthog, waterbuck and zebra.
Jozani Chwaka Bay National Park
Colobus monkey and duiker.
Katavi National Park
African wild dog, Cape buffalo, cheetah, crocodile, eland, elephant, giraffe, hartebeest, hippopotamus, hyena, impala, leopard, lion, reedbuck, roan antelope, sable antelope, topi, vervet monkey, vulture, waterbuck and zebra.
Kigosi & Moyowasi Game Reserve
Cape buffalo, bushbuck, crocodile, eland, elephant, hartebeest, hippopotamus, kudu, leopard, lion, roan antelope, sable antelope, serval cat, sitatunga antelope, topi, waterbuck and zebra.
Kitulo Plateau National Park
Eland, impala and reedbuck.

Kizigo Game Reserve

Baboon, bushbuck, bush pig, Cape buffalo, crocodile, dik-dik, duiker, eland, elephant, grysbok, hartebeest, hippopotamus, hyena, impala, jackal, kudu, klipspringer, leopard, lion, oribi, ostrich, reedbuck, roan antelope, sable antelope, serval cat, sitatunga antelope, steinbok, topi, warthog, waterbuck and zebra.

Lake Manyara National Park

Aardwolf, aardvark, African wild cat, baboon, blue monkey, bushbuck, Cape buffalo, civet cat, dik-dik, elephant, flamingo, giraffe, hippopotamus, impala, klipspringer, leopard, lion, mongoose, ostrich, pangolin, warthog, waterbuck, wildebeest and zebra.

Lukwika-Lumesule Game Reserve

African wild dog, antelope, baboon, bushbuck, bush pig, Cape buffalo, crocodile, duiker, eland, elephant, hippopotamus, impala, klipspringer, kudu, leopard, lion, reedbuck, roan antelope, sable antelope, suni, topi, warthog and waterbuck.

Mafia Island Marine Park

Bush pig, duiker, elephant shrew and mongoose.

Mahale Mountains National Park

Antelope, African wild dog, blue tailed monkey, bushbaby, Cape buffalo, chimpanzee, civet cat, colobus monkey, duiker, eland, elephant, giant squirrel, giraffe, hyrax, kudu, leopard, lion, mongoose, porcupine, red-tailed monkey, roan antelope, sable antelope, Sykes' monkey and vervet monkey.

Maswa Game Reserve

African wild dog, Cape buffalo, cheetah, eland, giraffe, Grant's gazelle, hartebeest, impala, leopard, lion, roan antelope, Thomson's gazelle, topi, waterbuck, wildebeest and zebra.

Mikumi National Park

African wild dog, antelope, baboon, Cape buffalo, cheetah, crocodile, eland, elephant, giraffe, hartebeest, hippopotamus, hyena, impala, jackal, kudu, leopard, lion, monitor lizard, python, rhinoceros (black), roan antelope, sable antelope, warthog, wildebeest and zebra.

Mkomazi Game Reserve

Aardvark, African wild dog, antelope, Cape buffalo, cheetah, crocodile, eland, elephant, gerenuk, giraffe, Grant's gazelle, hartebeest, hyena, jackal, kudu, leopard, lion, oryx, python, rhinoceros (black), steinbok, waterbuck, wild cat and zebra.

Mnazi Bay Ruvumba Estuary Marine Park

Crocodile and hippopotamus.

Msangesi Game Reserve (only accessible for private hunting July-December)

Cape buffalo, crocodile, elephant, klipspringer, leopard, lion, reedbuck and sable antelope.

Muhesi Game Reserve

Baboon, bushbuck, bush pig, Cape buffalo, crocodile, dik-dik, duiker, eland, elephant, grysbok, hartebeest, hippopotamus, hyena, impala, jackal, kudu, klipspringer, leopard, lion, oribi, ostrich, reedbuck, roan antelope, sable antelope, serval cat, sitatunga antelope, steinbok, topi, warthog, waterbuck and zebra.

Mt Kilimanjaro National Park

African wild dog, antelope, blue monkey, bushbuck, Cape buffalo, colobus monkey, duiker, eland, elephant, flamingo, leopard and oryx.

Ngezi Forest Reserve

Civet cat, colobus monkey, duiker, feral pig, hyrax, mongoose, pemba flying fox and vervet monkey.

Ngorongoro Conservation Area

African wild dog, baboon, bat-eared fox, bushbuck, Cape buffalo, cheetah, dik-dik, eland, elephant, giraffe, Grant's gazelle, hartebeest, hippopotamus, hyena, impala, jackal, leopard, lion, ostrich, reedbuck, rhinoceros (black), serval cat, Thomson's gazelle, vervet monkey, warthog, waterbuck, wildebeest and zebra.

Ruaha National Park

African wild dog, antelope, bushbuck, Cape buffalo, cheetah, civet cat, crocodile, dik-dik, eland, elephant, giraffe, Grant's gazelle, hartebeest, hippopotamus, hyena, impala, jackal, kudu, leopard, lion, mongoose, ostrich, reedbuck, roan antelope, sable antelope, rhinoceros (black & white), warthog, waterbuck and zebra.

Rubondo Island National Park

Antelope, bushbuck, chimpanzee, colobus monkey, crocodile, elephant, genet cat, flamingo, hippopotamus, jackal, lion, mongoose, otter, sitatunga antelope, suni, vervet monkey and zebra.

Rumanyika Game Reserve

Antelope, buffalo, eland and elephant.

Rungwa Game Reserve

Baboon, bushbuck, bush pig, Cape buffalo, crocodile, dik-dik, duiker, eland, elephant, grysbok, hartebeest, hippopotamus, hyena, impala, jackal, kudu, klipspringer, leopard, lion, oribi, ostrich, reedbuck, roan antelope, sable antelope, serval cat, sitatunga antelope, steinbok, topi, warthog, waterbuck and zebra.

Saa Nane Game Reserve

Hippopotamus, wildebeest and zebra.

Saadani National Park

Baboon, Cape buffalo, civet cat, colobus monkey, crocodile, duiker, eland, elephant, flamingo, giraffe, hartebeest, hippopotamus, hyena, kudu, leopard, lion, mongoose, reedbuck, sable antelope, serval cat, warthog, waterbuck, wildebeest and zebra.

Selous Game Reserve
African wild dog, antelope, bushbuck, Cape buffalo, cheetah, crocodile, eland, elephant, giraffe, hartebeest, hippopotamus, hyena, impala, klipspringer, kudu, leopard, lion, reedbuck, rhinoceros (black), sable antelope, warthog, waterbuck, wildebeest and zebra.

Serengeti National Park
Aardvark, African wild dog, baboon, bat-eared fox, bushbuck, Cape buffalo, cheetah, crocodile, colobus monkey, dik-dik, duiker, mongoose, eland, elephant, giraffe, Grant's gazelle, hartebeest, hippopotamus, hyena, hyrax, impala, jackal, klipspringer, leopard, lion, mongoose, oribi, oryx, ostrich, patas monkey, python, reedbuck, rhinoceros (black), roan antelope, serval cat, Thomson's gazelle, topi, warthog, waterbuck, wildebeest, vervet monkey and zebra.

Tarangire National Park
Baboon, bat-eared fox, Cape buffalo, cheetah, civet cat, dik-dik, eland, elephant, gazelle, gerenuk, giraffe, Grant's gazelle, ground squirrel, hartebeest, hyena, hyrax, impala, kudu, leopard, lion, mongoose, oryx, ostrich, porcupine, python, reedbuck, steinbok, python, rhinoceros, Thomson's gazelle, vervet monkey, warthog, waterbuck, wildebeest and zebra.

Udzungwa Mountains National Park
African wild dog, baboon, bushbuck, bush pig, Cape buffalo, chameleon, civet cat, red colobus monkey, duiker, eland, elephant, hippopotamus, honey badger, hyrax, klipspringer, leopard, lion, mongoose, pangolin, sable antelope, mangabey, squirrel and water buck.

Ugalla River Game Reserve
African wild dog, bushbuck, chimpanzee, crocodile, eland, elephant, hippopotamus, kudu, leopard, lion, oryx, roan antelope, sable antelope, topi and waterbuck.

Umba River Game Reserve
Blue monkey, elephant, gerenuk, kudu, oryx and rhinoceros (black).

Uwanda Game Reserve
Antelope, Cape buffalo, crocodile, eland, elephant, giraffe, hippopotamus, impala, kudu, reedbuck, roan antelope, topi and zebra.

The Maasai

The Maasai are a primitive, semi-nomadic, pastoralist tribe of Nilotic-Hamitic origin that inhabit the semi-arid and arid lands of the Great Rift Valley in Kenya and Tanzania.

The Maasai are predominantly a warrior tribe whose lives revolve around their livestock—cattle in particular. They believe that when the Earth and sky were divided, the rain god Ngai gave the Maasai tribe cattle, and with it the right to steal from other neighbouring tribes. A man's wealth in Maasai society is measured by the number of cattle and children he possesses.

The Maasai believe that the ground is sacred and they do not dig up the earth to cultivate crops, search for water or bury their dead. They are particularly dependent upon cattle for providing meat, blood and milk for daily sustenance. Piercing the jugular vein (in the cow's neck) with an arrow allows blood to be collected in a calabash (bowl). Milk is then added to prevent the warm blood from coagulating. Moistened cow dung is used to seal the open wound over the jugular vein. If a cow is slaughtered the Maasai carefully cut up the animal and apportion the best cuts of meat to individual men based on their seniority. Whatever remains is given to the women.

Loss of land to national parks and game reserves has reduced the Maasai's access to essential water supplies, fresh pastures and salt licks, and they now face the ongoing problems associated with drought and famine. In order to survive they either buy food, grow their own crops or sadly have become dependent upon foreign aid.

Maasai Society

Maasai society is patriarchal. Women are inferior, subservient and live a life of cultural oppression. At birth they become a member of their father's family line. When a female Maasai reaches puberty, her father chooses her a husband — who is usually much older—in exchange for cattle or cash. She becomes one of many wives and will continue to produce children for as long as she is able. A woman is not allowed to divorce her husband, she has no inheritance rights and is not allowed to own land or cattle. If her husband dies she becomes the property of her husband's brothers.

Rising early in the morning, it is the woman's daily duty to milk the cows, sweep the huts inside and out, prepare and cook food for the men, repair the cracked hut walls as and when necessary, and walk whatever distance is necessary to collect firewood and water.

Maasai men are warriors and it is their duty to guard and protect their tribe, livestock and pastures. Taking the cattle, goats and sheep out each morning, they may trek many kilometres in their relentless search for fresh grass and water. When grass and water are plentiful the elders will sit and watch the *layonis* (young boys who are not yet circumcised) herding the cattle. When food is scarce the *morans* (warriors) take over from the layonis moving the cattle further afield. The elders then visit friends in nearby *manyattas* (a group of huts that is temporary settlement), drink beer or let the women tend to their needs while they sit and wait for the morans to return before sundown. Morans who remain behind will either go hunting, visit nearby manyattas or play with the *nditos* (young girls). When food is scarce due to drought conditions, or when the pastures are exhausted of food from over grazing, the Maasai are forced to move on necessitating the construction of a new manyatta.

Manyattas

Small manyattas consist of up to ten huts. Large manyattas consist of up to 250 huts. Manyattas may or may not have a perimeter hedge.

It is the man's responsibility to construct the circular perimeter hedge that surrounds the village mud huts. This keeps the livestock and Maasai safe inside, and keeps predators out during the night. The hedge stands six feet high and is made from sticks, tree

223

branches and acacia thorn bushes. Up to four gates are present, which are opened early in the morning and closed at evening time.

It is the woman's responsibility to construct the mud huts, a task that can take up to seven months to complete. Traditional Maasai huts are constructed of upright tree branches with intertwining branches, sticks and twigs that are plastered and held together with mixture of mud, ash, grasses, cow dung and cow urine. This crude plaster is baked dry in the sun. Cracks appear regularly in the mud walls and the women and children are constantly repairing them. Ventilation holes are necessary to allow the smoke from cooking to escape, and these are located either in the roof or the outside walls. The presence of smoke deters disease-ridden mosquitoes or other pesky insects from entering the hut. The door is either made from wood or wickerwork, and in some instances a padlock may be present. The roof is dome-shaped and covered with layer upon layer of dried grass.

Each wife has her own mud hut, with a bed for her and her children. There is also a second bed in each hut for the husband, who will circulate round his wives. When the children are three to four years old they move into another hut. The beds are constructed of a wooden frame, straddled with an animal hide. Alternatively some Maasai sleep on the earthen floor.

Male Circumcision

The main Maasai celebrations are: birth, circumcision, the election of leaders and funerals.

Circumcision is the most important ritual conducted in Maasai society. This is when a boy becomes a man, entering the adult world of the morans or warrior class and earning the respect of the Maasai. Circumcision is known as *emurata* and takes place every seven years.

Each seven-year period is given a name and boys who are circumcised together are known to each other as age mates. Within each age group there will be a nominated leader under which there are junior leaders. They hold these positions of authority throughout their lives.

Young boys who are not circumcised are known as layonis and are of low status, having a life of hard, manual labour. They are well disciplined and respectful of their elders, only speaking when spoken to. When they meet an elder they bow their heads in respect so that the elder can place his hand on their scalp. The layoni is well-informed and knowledgeable about Maasai beliefs, culture and traditions.

The process begins with the elders asking the boys if they are ready to be circumcised. If agreement is reached, preparations to make beer (*anaiho*) from honey, sugar and water commence. After fermenting for three days the roots of the aloe plant are added and the process of fermentation continues for another two weeks.

On the afternoon before the day of circumcision the warriors commence dancing and singing with the boys who are due to be circumcised and this continues on into the night.

On the morning of the circumcision the boys' heads are shaved and the morans take them out into the bush and wash them down with cold water. This process is known as *engare endolu*. The boys return to their homes in silence and are greeted at the entrance to the *boma* (livestock enclosure), by the witch doctor. The boys are circumcised one at time. The boys are then escorted to the tea house and put to bed, where they drink a cocktail of blood and milk to revive them. A dedicated moran is in attendance for the next 7-14 days while the boys recover. If a boy refuses to be circumcised, it will result in him being bullied, tormented and ridiculed for the rest of his life. They are not allowed to be circumcised in a hospital under modern medical conditions, neither are they allowed any form of pain relief. Many are quite ill after the procedure has taken place and need to resort to a course of antibiotics to clear up any infections.

225

The boys post-circumcision are known as *skolio* and will spend the next seven to twelve months in small groups, visiting each other's manyattas. They wear black cloth, paint their faces black with white stripes and adorn their hair with feathers. Boys who were particularly brave during the circumcision process are allowed to wear head dresses made from ostrich or eagle feathers as a symbol of their bravery.

After this period another celebration takes place. The skolio becomes a junior moran and is allowed to grow his hair long, plaiting it into braids and smearing it with ochre and fat. He is also allowed to wear the traditional red cloth (*shuka*), which he drapes around his body. The morans from the preceding age group now become senior morans.

The boys progress after circumcision through a hierarchy of grades starting out initially as junior warriors, and progressing to senior warriors, junior elders and later senior elders. Senior elders are allowed to make the decisions that affect the whole tribe. In Maasai society each group lasts for about 15 years and each has unique responsibilities and codes of dress.

Female Circumcision

Female circumcision, or female genital mutilation as it is now commonly called, is illegal but still takes place in certain locations. It is believed that carrying out this procedure will reduce promiscuity and make child birth easier. Circumcision involves the partial or total removal of the female external genitalia. It is carried out by either an older woman or a female witch doctor, without anaesthetic. Female circumcision can lead to a lifetime of health problems and in some cases can be fatal.

When the circumcision is complete the two morans will hand the girl their spears as a signal that the process is finished and that she must now get up. The two morans then join in the dancing outside, and the girl must come out of the hut and hand the two spears back. She then returns to the hut to recover for a period of up to four months. Celebrations continue through the night. During the recovery period the newly circumcised girls are dressed in black and are referred to as *eskolio*. When they are fully recovered, which can take between seven to twelve months, they are referred to as *esingiki*, after which they can get married.

Maasai women are easily identified by their shaven heads, bright clothing and beads, and the removal of one of the bottom teeth.

Trivia

♦Long hair is a sign of beauty in a man and a shaven head is a sign of beauty in a woman.

♦Male and female Maasai pierce and stretch their earlobes. Long earlobes and cuts on the sides of the face of a woman are a sign of beauty. The tops and sides of the ears on both sexes may also be pierced and have metal rings inserted.

♦A Maasai man can have up to 20 wives.

♦Milk obtained from the cows is separated into three lots: one is drunk as fresh milk, another is mixed with cow's blood and another is left to go sour.

♦Wood ash and cow's urine are used to sterilise the calabash in which cow's blood is collected.

♦The Maasai use dried cow dung as fuel for their fires.

♦When a woman dies, her sons will anoint her body with sheep fat. Her body is then placed under a tree some distance from the manyatta. An animal skin is attached to an overhanging branch so that her eyes are covered to prevent vultures from pecking them out, and her body is left for the hyenas to devour during the night.

Insider Tips

Although outside the scope of this book, it would be remiss of us not to share with you some of the personal experiences that have enhanced our safaris in East Africa over the years.

Cultural Tourism Programmes

Cultural Tourism Programmes (CTPs) are unique to Tanzania but unfortunately have not yet caught on in Kenya, although judging by the increasing success story in Tanzania there is no doubt that Kenya will soon realise their value. In our opinion, CTPs are probably the best idea to hit Tanzania in recent years, and we strongly recommend that you take time to book some sort of itinerary with one of the many local organisations that exist throughout the traditional safari tourism areas.

The first CTP originated in 1995 and the basic idea was that when tourists had completed their safari and the safari companies had relieved them of their hard-earned cash (although in many cases perhaps not so hard-earned!), then the safari company would add on an activity provided by local people that involved cultural experiences and traditional activities. These activities were relatively inexpensive when compared with safari costs and the money paid went directly to the local people who provided the experience.

A typical example would be a half-day village walk and banana beer brewery visit, or an overnight stay in a Maasai village. Over the years these visits have become increasingly successful, not only through the income they generated for local people, but also because many tourists found that they enjoyed their 'cultural experience' more than the actual safari. As a result CTPs have been set up in more and more locations, and with an increased diversity of experiences offered.

Although we strongly recommend that any visitor to Tanzania books some type of activity with a Cultural Tourism Programme, we have to offer the obligatory word of caution with regard to the possibility of being ripped off—while it is sad that we have to warn of this when speaking of local inhabitants rather than corrupt officials and politicians, the underlying factor is that money is far too powerful in East Africa and temptation is often difficult to avoid, even if you are a genuine and hard-working local inhabitant. However, the vast majority of CTPs are genuine, honest, excellent value for money and can provide you with truly meaningful and life-enhancing experiences.

If we were to recommend any activities in particular, then top of the list would be a four-day Crater Highlands Trek starting at Nainokanoka and finishing at Engerasero. En route you visit the Empakaai Crater, the slopes of Ol Doinyo Lengai (an active volcano) and one night is spent camping at the infamous Acacia Bush Camp—the most remote and desolate place on earth we have ever spent a night at. Your camping equipment and food are carried by donkeys and you are accompanied throughout by a Maasai donkey handler and an armed ranger. An easier

option, but just as memorable, is a four-day hike through the lush and verdant West Usambara Mountains, starting and finishing at Lushoto. You are accompanied by a local guide, with accommodation and food being provided by local villagers. Our final recommendation, and the easiest in terms of physical effort, is a half-day walk through the sugar plantations of Mgaba in the South Pare Mountains. A local villager will take you for a leisurely stroll through the valley, where you will see life as it really is in this remote part of Tanzania, and you can even meet a real witchdoctor. To add to the experience, spend a night at Hill Top Tona Lodge with the highly-informative Mr Elly Kimbwereza as your host.

Meserani Snakepark

Originally a campsite set up on dry, arid scrubland just outside Arusha by a couple from South Africa, this has developed into a quite amazing compound offering so much for local and international visitors alike. Barry and Lynn Bale, (known to worldwide travellers as BJ and Ma), bought the land back in 1993 and through careful planting and much hard work they have developed it into what can only be described as a true oasis in the desert.

Within their compound there is:

♦A campsite, used mostly by independent travellers and overland truck groups. Without doubt it is the favourite campsite of any group that we take to East Africa, and a personal favourite of ours.

♦One of the most atmospheric bars in Tanzania.

♦A Maasai Culture Museum (an absolute must—the number of local schools who take their children there is testament to the quality of the experience).

♦A comprehensive collection of reptiles (including spitting cobras, black mambas and huge crocodiles).

♦Snakes and crocodiles that you can actually handle yourself.

♦Camel rides to a local Maasai village.

♦However, what is so very special about BJ and Ma is the way that they have dedicated their lives to helping the local Maasai population—they provide free emergency healthcare in their medical centre (including expensive anti-snake venom), an orphanage, support for local schools, and they provide employment and self-help opportunities for many of the local population. BJ and Ma are indeed true saints. Feel free to visit their website—www.meseranisnakepark.com

West Usambara Mountains

Previously recommended in the section on Cultural Tourism Programmes as a superb area for easy-level trekking, the Usambara Mountains are quite exceptional as a place just to visit and experience a contrast in culture and climate. Often quoted as the most friendly area of Tanzania, it is also the most densely populated, and because the mountain climate is so different to that of the plains below, you will experience a way of life that is seen by few visitors to Tanzania. The town of Soni should be your first port of call, and a stay at Maweni Farm is recommended. Lushoto is the largest town in the Usambaras, and it is here that the highly recommended Cultural Tourism Programme is based (their office is just behind the NMB Bank). If you can handle the surreal architecture of Irente View Cliff Lodge, then you will certainly be impressed as you stand on your four-wheel-drive bonnet and watch the early morning mist rise up out of the Rift Valley.

Tarangire National Park

One of the national parks normally visited as part of the 'Northern Circuit' of parks in Tanzania, Tarangire is often missed out in the shorter safari itineraries in favour of the Serengeti and the Ngorongoro Crater. This is good news for those who do seek out this delightful park because you see more wildlife than Land Rovers, and not vice versa as is too often the case in the more popular parks. Tarangire has an abundant elephant population, and is the ideal place to just sit and watch how they behave. We are forever intrigued by the way they interact with each other, and also how they interact with their physical environment—in Tarangire you have the chance to actually witness it all on your own and not in a convoy of four-wheel-drives. Your travel company will have selected your accommodation for you, but if you do have any say in the matter then we would recommend Tarangire Safari Lodge—although expensive, it is probably the cheapest lodge in the park, and the views from the communal terrace and from your static tent are worth every penny.

Lake Nakuru National Park

Not known for its abundance of wildlife, and often missed out by safari companies in favour of the Maasai Mara, Lake Nakuru National Park has actually provided us with some of our most memorable wildlife experiences. Because of its relatively low public profile, you will not be fighting with convoys of vehicles for the best vantage point, and your experiences with the wildlife are usually enjoyed on your own. There are white rhinos in abundance, and if you time it right you will not fail to be impressed by the thousands of pink flamingos. If you are camping, persuade your guide to use Makalia Falls campsite.

Nairobi National Park

How many millions of people over the years will have flown into Nairobi and never realised that there is an easily accessible national park literally minutes from the airport? Well worth a visit, you will see many species of African wildlife, and you may even spot some of the big five. Nairobi Animal Orphanage and Nairobi Safari Walk are in the grounds, and close by are the David Sheldrick Elephant Sanctuary and the AFEW Giraffe Centre.

Ol Pejeta Conservancy

As an alternative to Kenya's National Parks, Ol Pejeta offers all the wildlife you would expect, including the 'big five', but has fewer visitors, making your game drive a much more meaningful experience. Among the many extra attractions available in the conservancy is the opportunity to meet Baracka, the blind Black Rhino.

Hells Gate National Park

This park, close to Naivasha in Kenya's Rift Valley, offers you the rare and unmissable opportunity to go on a bicycle safari and a gorge expedition, all in one visit.

Crater Lake Sanctuary

From Hells Gate National Park, if you take the road west as it skirts round Lake Naivasha, you will eventually find signs to Crater Lake Sanctuary. As you wander round this game sanctuary on foot, you may well have it all to yourself—apart that is, from the giraffes, zebras, buffalo, an impressive range of antelopes and even aardvarks. Walk up to the crater rim, and gaze down into the green soda lake at the bottom of the extinct volcano. The Tented Camp that you can see below is as good as it looks, and having spent New Year's Eve there we cannot think of a better place to start the year, it is without doubt our favourite place in Africa, (the secret's out!). Their guided walks are highly recommended, and a night-time game drive is one of the most wonderful experiences we have ever shared together.

DIY 'Self-Drive' Safaris

Organising a safari trip on your own, which would involve hiring a self-drive vehicle and being self-sufficient inside a national park, is something that we would not recommend unless you are very experienced and supremely confident. While it is actually the only way that we ourselves now wish to travel in Kenya and Tanzania, it presents many potential hazards, and unless you know exactly what you are doing, you are putting your personal safety under unnecessary risk. However, it is becoming increasingly popular, and our next publication is devoted entirely to this very subject.

If you do ever embark on putting your own self-drive safari together, the most important piece of advice we can offer is that you hire a reliable four-wheel-drive vehicle, with a company that is capable of responding appropriately should you need assistance. We ourselves have used Central Rent a Car, Nairobi, and Fortes Safaris, Arusha, and have had no complaints. We have only needed urgent assistance on a couple of occasions, both in Tanzania, and the response from Fortes certainly exceeded our expectations.

Kupenda Africa

If you do wish to avoid joining the mass tourism bandwagon and actually organise your own visit to East Africa, but would like the safety net of someone else taking on the responsibility of putting your itinerary together, then put yourself in the hands of Grace M'mungania and Jason Smith of *Kupenda Africa*. Grace and Jason run their own company, providing group and family trips to Africa, and we cannot recommend them highly enough. When we take groups of students on overland expeditions to Kenya and Tanzania ourselves, we would not dream of using anyone else to cater for our specific requirements while we are there, whether it be the use of their overland truck, taking us into the Kibera Slum or introducing us to further unique and meaningful experiences. Although Grace and Jason offer incredible value for money, the main incentive behind letting them look after you is their passion for the people of East Africa—they will take you to places that the big companies do not bother with, and they will introduce you to experiences that will not necessarily increase their

233

profit margin, but will make you fall in love with Africa—its landscape, its wildlife and its people. Take a look at their website, www.kupendaafrica.com, and feel free to get in touch with them to see what they can do for you.

Guidebooks
Our constant companions when we plan our visits to Kenya and Tanzania, and the initial inspiration for many of our adventures, are the *Rough Guide* and *Lonely Planet* editions for both countries.

After sharing our East African 'treasures' with you, some words of caution—all based on our own personal experiences.

Choosing a safari company
If you have booked a package deal with a tour company then the choice of safari company is beyond your control. However, if you find yourself in a position where you are booking a safari direct with a company, then it is a potential minefield. The ubiquitous warnings about tourists being ripped off by bogus companies and 'budget safaris' should be well heeded.

A whole section of this book could be devoted to providing advice on how to avoid being ripped off, but we would simply be regurgitating the advice offered in the *Rough Guide* and *Lonely Planet* guidebooks, so we are strongly recommending that you read one of these publications and follow its advice.

We ourselves once booked a Crater Highlands Trek through a company highly recommended in travel guides. The company had a superb website, and everything seemed in order right up to the day when we had arranged to hand over a substantial cash deposit to their representative in Arusha. We took the advice offered in the guidebooks and popped into the Tourist Office on Boma Road, Arusha, just to check the company out—were we glad that we did this! Our email contact with the company had been hijacked and we had actually been communicating with someone who had been systematically relieving tourists of their cash, and then disappearing into thin air. The Tourist Office were quite matter-of-fact about telling us, simply reinforcing to us how commonplace this problem is.

Park fees

On an organised safari arranged by your tour company your park fees are paid for you by the safari company, but if you have actually booked the safari yourself make sure that the guide does pay in full all park fees at the park entrance—it is not unknown for the guide to underpay and this could cause you immense problems if your paperwork is checked by park representatives while you are inside the park.

If you are on a self-drive safari then you would be wise to check out the small print on park fees on the relevant park website. Make sure you know what you are paying for, and if you are travelling with children or students, look carefully for the appropriate discounts. In Tanzania national parks, once you have paid your 24-hour fee you are allowed to leave the park (for cheaper overnight accommodation), and then return the next morning to complete your full 24 hours. In Kenya's national parks your 24-hour allowance only allows you to leave the park and return once, but be aware that in their Sanctuaries and in Lake Nakuru National Park your 24-hour allowance may cease once you leave the park (you may have to pay a re-entry fee, and some unscrupulous park employees will actually try to get you to pay the full fee again.)

Personal safety

Some areas of Kenya and Tanzania can be quite dangerous, for many different reasons. There are inherent dangers with regard to local crime, the environment and wild animals—you should actively seek the advice of your guide at all times.

Local transport

Using local transport is, in our opinion, the most hazardous component of any itinerary in Kenya or Tanzania. Serious traffic accidents in these two countries are commonplace and we witness them frequently. The ubiquitous *matatus* (minibuses that ply local routes) have a very poor safety record, although local authorities are doing their best to regulate their use. The large coaches that connect the major towns, and drive at breakneck speed irrespective of whatever is going on around them also have a poor safety record. If you do need to travel independently, then the shuttle buses that connect Nairobi to Arusha and Moshi are probably your best option. The most popular ones are Riverside Shuttle and Impala Shuttle—we use them just about every time we visit East Africa and have never had any problems.

When to go

People usually travel to Kenya and Tanzania to go on safari in the dry seasons, which are either December–March (short dry season) or July–October (long dry season). Avoid March–June (long rainy season) as the roads can become treacherous and impassable. The short dry season is very hot and can be uncomfortable, especially during the night when you need to be covered up to stop the mosquitoes biting you. The long dry season is much cooler and comfortable but can get quite cold in tent during the night. However, when you go is entirely up to you and may be dictated by budget.

Souvenirs

While on safari you will get the opportunity to visit the curio shops en route. Be aware that those visited as part of a safari package tend to be very expensive. You may wish to negotiate with your guide to visit the local curio markets or street markets instead, engage in some serious bartering and have lots of fun. You will also be helping the local economy.

Tipping

Your guides, drivers and cooks will be paid a wage by the safari company, but this is invariably very poor. The safari company will usually tell you that you are expected to pay the driver/guide something in the region of $20 per day and the cook $10 per day. This may come as a shock, particularly if you are on a lengthy trip, and you may not have budgeted appropriately. The problem is that because these people are paid such low wages by the safari companies, they really do rely heavily on tips to supplement their income. Your response to this predicament is a matter of your own choice, but if you do feel obliged to pay a tip, be aware of any pressure to give more than would be sensible and adequate.

Money

If using travellers cheques take the receipt from the bank in the UK with you as proof of evidence of purchase.

Only buy new US Dollars—notes more than 10 years old may not be accepted in Kenya and Tanzania because of fraud/counterfeit money.

Do not be tempted to exchange currency with locals, particularly those who harass you as you cross the border. Despite the favourable exchange rates you may be buying counterfeit money.

At the time of print, all contact details and other information above was known to be correct but may change with time.

The Meserani Project

We are donating all proceeds from the sale of this book to The Meserani Project—indeed, this project was a major inspirational factor when the idea behind the book first crossed our minds.

The Meserani Project is a registered charity, but is still regarded as a 'homegrown' project, set up by a secondary school in the heart of Middlesbrough, an urban town in the industrialised north-east of England. It all began in August 2004 when a group of pupils from Acklam Grange School became involved in some of the most impoverished schools in Tanzania and Kenya as part of a three-week overland camping expedition. Emotions overspilled when the pupils visited Lesiraa Primary School, in the Meserani District of Tanzania, and were confronted with wooden shacks that were literally falling apart, a complete lack of sanitation and a desperate shortage of even the most basic of educational resources such as pens and exercise books. What affected the pupils most however, were the wonderful and natural smiles that greeted us from every child—despite their desperate situation. The pupils felt that they could not simply walk away and turn their back on Lesiraa School, so vowed to set up a project when they returned to school in Middlesbrough, dedicated to making some sort of change at Lesiraa. The Lesiraa Project evolved, and pupils from Acklam Grange School raised enough money to build, furnish and equip four brand new classrooms at Lesiraa. In 2007 a second group of pupils from Acklam Grange School visited Lesiraa School as part of another overland camping expedition, and they were able to view the new classrooms themselves.

The second phase of the project was to rebuild Meserani Juu School, another primary school in the same district as Lesiraa School, also in dire need of decent classrooms and basic educational resources. The Acklam Grange pupils who witnessed Meserani Juu School in 2007 were shocked and distressed at what they saw, and made tearful promises to return to Middlesbrough and start fundraising all over again. Hence, the project now became known as The Meserani Project.

In 2009 a third group of pupils from Acklam Grange undertook a three-week overland camping expedition in Tanzania and Kenya, a major part of their visit being to work at Meserani Juu School. They were able to see for themselves the four new classrooms that had been built, and spent time painting murals on the outside walls, as well as engaging with the pupils and staff and organising a sports day for all pupils in the Meserani District. During their time in Kenya the pupils visited St. Secilia School, in Kibera, Nairobi—the largest slum area in Africa. The visits involved taking lessons, providing educational resources, sports equipment and stocks of food, and visiting some of the pupils in their homes inside the slum. A long-term aim of the project is to purchase a plot of land on the outskirts of the slum and build a brand new, purpose-built school for the St. Secilia pupils.

A fourth visit in 2011 led to the building of two classrooms at Meserani Chini Primary School, seven water tanks for two secondary boarding schools, solar power to a girls' boarding school and text books for the staff and pupils at two schools. The focus for the project now is to sponsor pupils from the Meserani Project to attend secondary school. Very few pupils in Tanzania complete their four years of secondary education, primarily because they have to pay. The Meserani Project is sponsoring 86 pupils from the Meserani District to go through their full four years of secondary education, with the first 9 starting at Einoti Secondary School in January 2009 followed by another 16 in January 2010. In January 2011 a further 28 pupils started their secondary education at Moita Boys Boarding School and Kipok Girls Boarding School, and 33 more started here in January 2012 —all sponsored by The Meserani Project. On the next page we have selected some phrases from the letters that some of the pupils from Meserani have sent to their sponsors in Middlesbrough.

Middlesbrough is known nationally for its depravation, whether it be high levels of absence from school, poor health, teenage pregnancies, drug abuse—or any other national statistic that the press makes known. The Meserani Project is Acklam Grange School's response. The pupils, staff and parents have united behind this project, and are determined to show what they can really achieve, given the opportunity. By purchasing this safari guide you also have made a contribution and we thank you for that.

In my daily life I was asking God every day to help me achieve my goal ... It was very difficult ... but I think God heard my voice. Thank you for agreeing to support me in my studies. With your help I promise that I will study hard. It was like a dream to be sponsored by somebody. I love you all because you are very important people in my life.
Stela

You are my mum and dad. I beg you please love me as your children because I have no peace in this Earth ... God bless you because without you I will fail to continue with my education.
Lelo

I don't have anything to pay or give you for your kindness. But I will pray to our Heavenly Father to keep you safe today, tomorrow and forever and ever ... and may He open all doors of blessing to you my sponsors. Never give up on helping me...
Theresia

I don't think I am an orphan. I feel that I still have my parents because you are the one who makes me feel that. You have taken my parents part and that is why I bring my thanks to you. I pray for you to God for all the things that you are doing for me...
Lucas

I have nothing to give you, but this letter ... It is unexplained joy to know that among the great numbers of Maasai girls who are suffering from various problems including not given the chance of education that I am released.
Leah

I thank you my sponsors because I face many problems and obstacles in my daily life and studies. My father has died and my mother is a widow. Thank you for helping me and relieving me of these problems because without you I would not be accepted to study or continue with secondary education...
Winnie

241

Fact Files

Altitude   Height above sea level.

Antlers   Bony protuberances that have a branch like structure on the front of the skull and are shed annually.

Aorta   Main major artery that carries blood away from the heart.

Asphyxiation   To lose consciousness due to lack of oxygen.

Arboreal   Tree dwelling. Spends the majority of life living in the trees, only coming to the ground on rare occasions.

Arid   Dry, desert environment with little or no rain

Biome   An extremely large ecosystem.

Browser   Animals that feed mainly on leaves but will eat twigs from low lying branches of trees and bushes.

Bulk grazers   Animals that are not selective about which grasses they eat.

Buoyancy   The ability to float or rise in water.

Caldera   Collapsed volcano.

Carcass   The dead body of an animal.

Carnivore   Meat-eating animal or bird.

Carrion   Dead, rotting flesh.

Caste system   A complex organisation made up of different social classes, who all perform different duties to the mutual benefit of the whole group.

Climate   Average weather conditions

Cloven–hoofed or even-toed ungulate   A hoof that splits into two or four toes (antelope, hippopotamus, giraffe, warthog).

Cognitive   Ability to acquire knowledge and reason.

Cold-blooded   Cold-blooded creatures are unable to generate their own body heat. Their body temperature is regulated by the temperature of the surrounding environment.

Contagious   A transmissible disease that is passed on by contact.

Crepuscular   Primarily active at dusk and dawn.

Cud   Partly digested food that an animal regurgitates back into its mouth to continue chewing.

Deforestation	A forested area that has been cleared by humans causing permanent damage to the ecosystem.
Desert	Annual rainfall is less than 25cm. Deserts may be hot or cold.
Desertification	When the climate of a dry region becomes even drier. The vegetation dies and is eaten by grazing animals leaving the soil vulnerable to the effects of erosion.
Diurnal	Active during the day and resting at night.
Dorsal	On the back.
Dorsum	Back of the body.
Drought	Shortage of water.
Ecosystem	A community of plants, animals and people that interact with the climate and soil.
Estivate	A period of dormancy similar to hibernation, but takes place when temperatures are high and conditions are dry.
Eviscerate	To disembowel - removal of internal organs/entrails.
Extinct volcano	A volcano that has erupted in the past but will not erupt again.
Faeces	Dung, excrement.
Family	An extended family that consists of the breeding pair, the latest litter, previous litter and adolescents.
Fauna	Animals that live within an ecosystem.
Fledge	To leave the nest.
Forage	Search for food.
Gazelle	A small antelope renowned for its beauty, elegance, gracefulness, agility and speed.
Gestation	The process of foetal development in the womb.
Grazer	Grazers feed only on grass on the ground.
Habituated	Accustomed to/used to.
Haemorrhaging	Prolific, intense bleeding.
Harem	A group of mammals that consists of one dominant male and a harem of females. The size of the harem varies from species to species.
Herbivore	Plant eater.
Hierarchy	A system where there is a graded order.
Horns	A permanent bony protuberance.
Hydrophobia	Fear of water.
Infanticide	The act of killing the young/offspring.
Infectious	A disease that is passed on without contact.

Infrasonic	Sound that is extremely low pitched and cannot be detected by the human ear.
Insectivore	A plant or animal that eats insects.
Iteroparous	Offspring are produced by more than one female and are incubated in one clutch.
Invertebrate	Does not possess a backbone.
Involuntarily	Automatically, spontaneously, unconsciously.
Keratin	Fibrous substance found in hair, nails, feathers and hooves.
Laterite	Soil that is highly weathered. The soil bakes in the sun and forms a hardened crust.
Latrine	Toilet.
Nocturnal	Active at twilight and throughout the night.
Nomadic	Migratory, moving from place to place.
Matriarch	Dominant female, usually the oldest and largest.
Midden	Dung heap. Informs intruders that the area is already occupied by an animal of the same species. An intruder entering the area is not welcome and may encounter aggressive behaviour. Occasionally they are tolerated if they remain subordinate and are not perceived as a threat.
Mixed feeders	Animals that graze and browse, feeding on a variety of vegetation.
Molar	A tooth usually place at the back of the mouth used for grinding and crushing food.
Monogamous	Only has one partner at a time. May form a breeding pair and may mate for life.
Musth	State of heightened sexual excitement in large, male mammals, particularly elephants.
Myocarditis	Inflamed heart muscle.
Natal	Of or relating to birth.
Nomad	A person who moves from place to place with no fixed abode.
Odd-toed ungulate	Odd toed ungulates have one or three toes.
Oestrus	Sexually receptive and fertile (female).
Old World	Refers to the Earth's eastern hemisphere and includes the continents of Africa, Asia, Australia and Europe.
Oligarchy	A complex social group dominated by one or more dominant males.
Omnivore	An animal that eats and digests vegetable and animal matter.

Orifice	Opening.
Ossified	Has changed into bone.
Oviparous	Eggs that are produced by the mother that hatch outside the body.
Ovoviviparous	A snake that produces soft eggs that break open at birth.
Parasite (Complete)	An animal or plant that lives in or on another animal or plant (host) and is totally dependent upon it for nutrients.
Parasite (Semi)	An animal or plant that lives in or on another animal or plant (host), and is partly dependent on it for nutrients.
Patriarchal	Male-dominated social structure.
Plain	A large area of flattened land.
Plasma	Clear fluid found in blood, which carries the platelets and red and white blood cells.
Platelet	A particle of blood necessary for clotting.
Polyandrous	Females having more than one male to mate with at one time.
Polygamous	Has more than one partner at the same time.
Polygon	Many sided figure.
Predator	An animal that kills and eats other animals.
Precipitation	Water that falls from the sky either as rain, snow, hail or sleet.
Prehensile	Has the ability to grasp an object.
Primate	A mammal with flexible hands and feet and a highly developed brain.
Raptor	A bird of prey.
Regurgitated	Partly digested food that is coughed up, usually to feed the young.
Ruminant	A mammal that chews its cud (goat, deer, cattle, giraffe, camel).
Rutting	Mating period (mammals).
Savanna(h)	Open grassland with scattered bushes or trees.
Scavenger	Feeds on the remains of plants or animals.
Scute	Horny or bony external plate or scale.
Selective grazers	Animals that eat specific grasses or plant matter.
Siblicide	The death of an individual caused by close relatives.
Sibling	Brother or sister.

Solitary animals	Adult animals that remain alone but only meet up to mate during the breeding season. Examples are snake, serval cat, leopard, black and white rhino and the caracal.
Species	Type of animal or plant.
Stereoscopic Vision	The field of vision of each eye overlaps and enables the individual to judge distances.
Symbiotic	Two different species that benefit from living together.
Retractable	Ability to withdraw inwards.
Talon	The sharply hooked claw of bird.
Tap root	The main root of a plant that goes downwards with offshoots that grow sideways.
Temperate Climates	Do not experience great extremes in temperature.
Temporary Associations	Animals that are not bonded to each other, usually leaderless and non-territorial.
Terrestrial	An animal that spends the majority of its life living on the land.
Territory	An area of land occupied by an animal or group of animals that do not share the resources with other animal of the same species.
Tropics	That part of the Earth that lies between the Tropic of Capricorn (23.5° south of the Equator) and the Tropic of Cancer (23.5° north of the Equator).
Ungulates	Mammals that have developed hooves to aid walking and running, instead of claws. Ungulates are terrestrial herbivores that graze on grass, seeds, leaves, fruit and herbs.
Vertebrate	Possesses a back bone.
Viviparous	Gives birth to live young.
Weaned	Has the ability to live on food, other than the mother's milk.
Xerophytic	Drought-resistant plant.

Collective Names for Animals

Antelope	Cluster, herd, tribe.
Baboon	Congress, flange, troop.
Bat-eared fox	Cloud, earth, group, leash, skulk, troop.
Buffalo	Gang, herd, obstinacy, troop.
Cheetah	Coalition.
Crocodile	Bask, congregation, float, nest.
Eland	Herd.
Elephant	Arrangement, crash, herd, memory, pack, parade.
Flamingo	Colony, flamboyance, flock, stand.
Grant's gazelle	Herd.
Giraffe	Corps, herd, journey, kaleidoscope, kindergarten, tower, troop.
Hartebeest	Herd.
Hippopotamus	Bloat, herd, pod, raft, school, thunder.
Hyena	Cackle, clan.
Hyraxe	Colony, harem, herd.
Impala	Clan, harem, herd.
Leopard	Leap, lepe, prowl.
Lion	Flock, pride, sault, sowse, troop.
Marabou stork	Colony.
Mongoose	Business .
Monkey	Barrel, carload, cartload, troop.
Ostrich	Flock, harem, herd, troop.
Rhinoceros	Crash, herd, stubbornness.
Snake	Bed, den, knot, nest, pit, tribe.
Termite	Brood, colony, nest, swarm.
Thomson's gazelle	Herd.
Topi	Herd.
Vulture	Carpet, cast, committee, drove, flock, herd, venue, wake.
Warthog	Sounder.
Waterbuck	Harem, herd.
Wildebeest	Herd, implausibility.
Zebra	Cohort/dazzle/harem/herd/zeal

Swahili Words List

Acacia tree	*Mgunga.*
Agama	*Mjusi kafiri.*
Antelope	*Swala.*
Baboon	*Nyani.*
Baobab tree	*Mbuyu tree.*
Bat-eared fox	*Mbweha masikio.*
Bird	*Ndege.*
Black mamba	*Koboko mweusi.*
Boomslang	*Kijoka, Kimkufu.*
Buffalo	*Nyati, Mbogo.*
Bushbuck	*Kulungu, mbawala.*
Chameleon	*Kinyonga.*
Cheetah	*Duma, Chita.*
Cobra	*Swira.*
Colobus monkey	*Mbega mweupe.*
Crocodile	*Mamba.*
Dik-dik	*Funo, Dikidiki, Digidigi, Dika mbwa, Dik dik.*
Dog	*Umbwa .*
Enclosure/Maasai village	*Boma.*
Eland	*Mpofu, Mbungu, Pofu.*
Elephant	*Tembo, Ndovu.*
Flamingo	*Heroe.*
Flat headed rock agama	*Mjusi Kafiri.*
Foot-and-mouth disease	*Ugonjwa wa midomo na miguu.*
Gabon viper	*Moma.*
Gazelle	*Swala.*
Genet cat	*Kanu.*
Giraffe	*Twiga.*
Grant's gazelle	*Swala granti.*
Green mamba	*Koboko kijani.*
Hartebeest	*Kongoni.*
Hippopotamus	*Kiboko, Nyamu ngunihi.*
Hyena	*Fisi.*
Hyrax	*Pimbi.*
Impala	*Swala pala.*
Jackal	*Bweha .*
Kudu	*Tandala.*
Marabou stork	*Batamaji.*
Monitor lizard	*Kenje.*
Monkey	*Tumbili.*
Leopard	*Chui.*

Lion	*Simba.*
Mongoose	*Nguchiro.*
Monitor lizard	*Kenge*
Oryx	*Choroa.*
Ostrich	*Mbuni.*
Python	*Chatu.*
Puff adder	*Kifutu.*
Rabies	*Kichaa cha mwba.*
Red-billed oxpecker bird	*Askari wa kiaru.*
Reedbuck	*Tohe.*
Rhinoceros	*Kifaru, Faru.*
Rinderpest	*Sotoka.*
Rock hyrax	*Pimbi.*
Sausage tree	*Mbura.*
Serengeti	*Siringit* (Maasai for "Endless Plains").
Snake	*Nyoka.*
Spider	*Buibui.*
Termites	*Mchwa.*
Thomson's gazelle	*Swala tomi.*
Ticks	*Kupe.*
Tree hyrax	*Perere.*
Vine snake	*Funga kuni.*
Vervet monkey	*Tumbili.*
Vulture	*Tai, Gushii.*
Warthog	*Ngiki, Ngiri, Gwasi.*
Waterbuck	*Kuro.*
Wild dog	*Mbwa mwitu.*
Wildebeest	*Nyumbu.*
Zebra	*Punda milia.*

Acknowledgments

Putting this guide together has been hard work; it has taken an incredible amount of time and has probably been the biggest challenge of our lives, but because it has involved our interaction with the people and animals of East Africa it has been great fun as well. While researching and writing this book numerous people have helped us along the way by providing advice, information and guidance, and we would like to take this opportunity to acknowledge their contributions.

We owe so much to Zoe Wildsmith as without her help and advice this book would not have been possible. Zoe has guided us from start to finish, initially giving practical advice on how to get started, then providing constant guidance and motivation as the book began to take shape, and finally editing and proofing the entire contents. Zoe has been inspirational to us both, and we thank her for that.

We are indebted to Chris Packham for taking time out of his busy schedule as a BBC Wildlife Presenter to write the foreword to the book.

Abigail Bell, former pupil at Acklam Grange School, Middlesbrough, has kindly provided all of the animal illustrations, which add further interest to the book. This took many hours, and we appreciate the personal sacrifices she made.

The following people have either read and commented on our work, advised us, or have sourced information for us: Barry (BJ) and Lynn (Ma) Bale—owners of Meserani Snake Park, Arusha, Tanzania; Loti Naparana—Senior Guide and Herpetologist at Meserani Snake Park; Jason and Grace of Kupenda Africa Travel Company; Andy Jones, Stephen Parker, Mike Riley, Rachael Grandey, Chris Joseph, Mark Crandon, Tom Chapman, Zac Laizer (deceased), Ruth Delany, Sarah Naylor, Stephanie Crandon, Liam Steinbeck (Berghaus); plus of course the numerous local guides whom we have had the pleasure of meeting on our travels out in the bush.

The majority of the photographs were taken by the authors, but the following friends have kindly allowed us to include their photographs: John Bate, Emma Wells, Neil Atkinson, Jenny Lister, Stephanie Crandon and Andrew McCullagh. Andrew came with us to East Africa when he was a secondary school pupil, and he tragically and unexpectedly passed away in his sleep while studying at university—his photograph of a lioness and her three cubs in the Ngorongoro Crater is a fitting tribute to a wonderful young man.

Travel Africa

A UK & East Africa Partnership – Your Africa Travel Resource
Private Hire, Tour Holidays and Expedition Assistance for
Groups / Families / Companies / Schools / Clubs etc.

Specialising in East Africa Travel and Adventure
Kenya – Uganda – Rwanda – Tanzania
Including Trips from East Africa through Malawi, Zambia, Zimbabwe
Overland Trucks & 4 x 4 Travel & Guidance

Adventure e.g.
Mountain Gorilla Trekking in Rwanda/Uganda
Masai Mara & possibly The Great Migration
Serengeti & Ngorongoro Crater
Climb MT Kenya – MT Kilimanjaro
Bungee, Jet Boat, Canoe and White Water Raft the Nile
Zanzibar Island for cocktails, Scuba, snorkelling, spices, beaches
Or travel around Lake Victoria and experience all the above
Cultural e.g.
Stay in a village and experience coffee and tea picking
Visits to schools, orphanages, different tribes, local entertainment
Accommodation e.g.
Hotels, Lodges, Static Safari Tents, Camping or a mix of any

Please email with any ideas or queries you may have
www.kupendaafrica.com – jason@kupendaafrica.com
Kupenda Africa means 'To Love Africa' in Swahili

Made in the USA
Las Vegas, NV
26 December 2022

64132506R00150